# YOUR GUIDE TO BIG GAME HUNTING

## IN THE UNITED STATES

by
Kenneth A. Meyer, Jr.

Purple Mountain Outdoor Specialists
P.O. Box 2835
Evergreen, CO 80437-2835

www.PurpleMtnOS.com

Library of Congress
Card Catalog Number 00-192042

ISBN 0-9672039-1-0

Cover Design by TLC Unlimited - www.TLCUnlimited.com

Dedication

This book is dedicated to the memory of following individuals for their guidance and companionship enjoying the outdoors:

Carl "Skeeter" Blankenship, Jr,
Henry "Hiney" Bunge
Delbert "Bill" Bickford
Leonard Forsee
Tex Frank
Jim Jarvis
Landon Koelling
Armin Meyer
Ed Kokesh
Roger Krechel
Wilbur "Jiggs" Muschany
Frederick "Cedric" Sprick
Roy Sudbrock

## Disclaimer

Hunting big game requires the use of firearms, knives, and other sharp objects and may require strenuous activity. As such, this activity should be considered inherently dangerous and Purple Mountain Outdoor Specialists and the author cannot be held liable for any incident, accident, loss, or injury to any reader while hunting or preparing to hunt big game.

# Table of Contents

# 1

# Introduction

Big game hunting is a tradition enjoyed by millions of men and women throughout the United States. We are blessed to have well-managed game populations and endless possibilities for enjoying the outdoors.

Every year, hunters gather in deer camps in the northeast, ranches and leases in the south, on farms in the Midwest, and in camps on the prairie, in the mountains and on the tundra to pursue deer, elk, antelope, bear, moose, sheep, goat, and caribou. These hunts represent a significant commitment of time, effort, and often, money. The success and enjoyment of these hunts depends on a variety of factors including pre-hunt planning, equipment, supplies, and preparation.

**Chapter 2** provides valuable information for planning a big game hunt. Topics such as forming a hunting group, selecting a hunting location, establishing a budget, using guides vs. do-it-yourself hunts, and participating in drawing hunts are discussed.

**Chapter 3** identifies critical gear for different hunting situations and helps you select the right gear for your hunt. From remote tent camps to hunting the back '40, items such as tents, sleeping bags, clothing, and survival gear can make your experience more enjoyable and safer. Lists to assist with planning and tips for selecting a good campsite are provided.

**Chapter 4** covers a topic near and dear to every hunter's heart - food! Planning ahead and buying the right quantities and types of food will save you time and money. It also ensures that everyone in your camp is well-fed and satisfied with the quality and quantity of food served. Easy, delicious recipes give meal tips and sample menus help with planning. Cooking gear is also discussed.

**Chapter 5** addresses preparing for and enjoying the hunt. Proper personal preparation is important to maximize enjoyment and success potential. Tips for enjoying the hunt more are included.

**Chapter 6** includes contact information and summary discussions for all 50 states. Suggestions are included on when and where to go. Contact information is also provided for the U.S. Forest Service and the Bureau Of Land Management.

# 2

# Planning

Proper planning is essential to a successful big game hunt. Knowing the opportunities available - game types, methods, seasons, hunting locations, guides and outfitters, etc. is critical. Equally important is getting the right group together for the hunt. This chapter provides strategies to help you discover the right opportunities for your hunt and gives some guidelines for forming a compatible group.

## Forming a Hunting Group

Forming a hunting group can be a formidable task - potentially as stressful as finding a spouse or a new job. Selecting the right group to hunt with typically has more to do with enjoying your hunting experience than the animals taken. When forming a hunting group or being asked to join an existing group, think about your position on the following subjects before deciding:

- Safety and overall attitude towards hunting - Are you more concerned about partying or seriously focused on hunting? Is safety everyone's primary concern?

- Type of hunting on this trip - Will you be stand hunting, still hunting, driving, using dogs or bait, etc.? Is this an archery (muzzleloader, rifle) only hunt? Be sure you are comfortable with the hunting methods.

- What are the physical demands of the hunt? Setting in a blind or stand in warm weather? Climbing 5000 vertical feet up steep, rocky slopes everyday? Chasing hounds through swampy terrain? Backpacking into remote areas? Don't agree to a hunt unless you understand what is required to be successful and you are physically and mentally capable of enjoying the hunt.

- What are the accommodations? Will you be staying in tents, a camper, cabin, motel, someone's home, etc.? Some people consider it roughing it if they can't get cable tv. Be sure you understand where and what you'll be eating.

- What are the costs? License costs, trespass fees, food, gas, and lodging costs should all be considered.

- What happens with the game? Does everyone take their own? Is the meat split evenly amongst the party? How is game retrieved from the field? How will the meat be stored/cared for until the trip is over?

Group size is another important consideration. Some folks prefer to hunt in large groups - up to 20 or more. Others prefer smaller groups - two to six. Each approach has pros and cons. Large groups have more difficult logistics (cooking, area to hunt, etc.) but also have more hands to do the work. Smaller groups are easier to cook for and find hunting space for, but less strong backs are available for retrieving game. Identify your own preferences and avoid those situations that make you uncomfortable.

When forming a hunting party, writing your thoughts down on these issues down can help explain your plan to others. If they are agreeable, ask them to join. If not, keep looking. If you are asked to join a group, ask the same questions and agree to join only if their thoughts and approach to the trip are compatible with yours. Remember, you'll be spending precious hunting time with this group, be sure they have the same understanding and expectations that you do. I'd rather pass on an opportunity than spend a week or more being miserable with a group of hunters that I have almost nothing in common with.

## Selecting A Location

Many hunting camps are held in traditional locations, sometimes for several generations. Information on how and where to hunt are handed down to new members of the group. Stand locations and geographical features may be named - "I'm going to hunt the old cemetery stand today." Hunting in this type of situation is relatively simple - you know where you're going and how you'll be hunting.

Picking a new place and/or a new species to hunt can be intimidating. Your trip may involve a drive halfway across the country, hunting in unfamiliar terrain, for an animal with totally different behavior than you are used to. The best way to overcome the uncertainty associated with such a commitment is to plan it out carefully, as far in advance as possible. If you're forming a group, writing it down is a good way to be sure everyone understands what they are signing up for. Try to limit your group size during these planning stages - it can be difficult to agree on a location and hunt type with more than three or four people.

The first step is to decide on the species you'll be hunting. The following table can be used to guide you in locating what state your game of choice is hunted in.

# Big Game Selection Table

| | Antelope | Axis Deer | Barbary Sheep | Bear | Bighorn Sheep | Bison | Blacktail Deer | Caribou | Dall Sheep | Desert Bighorn | Elk | Feral Goat | Feral Sheep | Ibex | Mouflon Sheep | Mountain Goat | Moose | Mule Deer | Musk OX | Oryx | Whitetail Deer |
|---|---|---|---|---|---|---|---|---|---|---|---|---|---|---|---|---|---|---|---|---|---|
| Alabama | | | | | | | | | | | | | | | | | | | | | X |
| Alaska | | | | X | | X | X | X | X | | X | | | | | X | X | | X | | |
| Arizona | X | | | X | X | X | | | | X | X | | | | | | | X | | | X |
| Arkansas | | | | X | | | | | | | X | | | | | | | | | | X |
| California | X | | | X | | | X | | | X | X | | | | | | | X | | | |
| Colorado | X | | | X | X | | | | | X | X | | | | | X | X | X | | | X |
| Connecticut | | | | | | | | | | | | | | | | | | | | | X |
| Delaware | | | | | | | | | | | | | | | | | | | | | X |
| Florida | | | | | | | | | | | | | | | | | | | | | X |
| Georgia | | | | X | | | | | | | | | | | | | | | | | X |
| Hawaii | | X | | | | | X | | | | | X | X | | X | | | | | | |
| Idaho | X | | | X | X | | | | | | X | | | | | X | X | X | | | X |
| Illinois | | | | | | | | | | | | | | | | | | | | | X |
| Indiana | | | | | | | | | | | | | | | | | | | | | X |
| Iowa | | | | | | | | | | | | | | | | | | | | | X |
| Kansas | X | | | | | | | | | | X | | | | | | | X | | | X |
| Kentucky | | | | | | | | | | | | | | | | | | | | | X |
| Louisiana | | | | | | | | | | | | | | | | | | | | | X |
| Maine | | | | X | | | | | | | | | | | | | X | | | | X |
| Maryland | | | | | | | | | | | | | | | | | | | | | X |
| Massachusetts | | | | X | | | | | | | | | | | | | | | | | X |
| Michigan | | | | X | | | | | | | X | | | | | | | | | | X |
| Minnesota | | | | X | | | | | | | X | | | | | | X | | | | X |
| Mississippi | | | | | | | | | | | | | | | | | | | | | X |
| Missouri | | | | | | | | | | | | | | | | | | | | | X |

# Big Game Selection Table (cont.)

| | Antelope | Axis Deer | Barbary Sheep | Bear | Bighorn Sheep | Bison | Blacktail Deer | Caribou | Dall Sheep | Desert Bighorn | Elk | Feral Goat | Feral Sheep | Ibex | Mouflon Sheep | Mountain Goat | Moose | Mule Deer | Musk OX | Oryx | Whitetail Deer |
|---|---|---|---|---|---|---|---|---|---|---|---|---|---|---|---|---|---|---|---|---|---|
| Montana | X | | | X | X | | | | | | X | | | | | X | X | X | | | X |
| Nebraska | X | | | | X | | | | | | X | | | | | | | X | | | X |
| Nevada | X | | | | X | | | | | X | X | | | | | X | | X | | | |
| New Hampshire | | | | X | | | | | | | | | | | | | X | | | | X |
| New Jersey | | | | | | | | | | | | | | | | | | | | | X |
| New Mexico | X | | X | X | X | | | | | X | X | | | X | | | | X | | X | |
| New York | | | | X | | | | | | | | | | | | | | | | | X |
| North Carolina | | | | X | | | | | | | | | | | | | | | | | X |
| North Dakota | X | | | | X | | | | | | X | | | | | | X | X | | | X |
| Ohio | | | | | | | | | | | | | | | | | | | | | X |
| Oklahoma | X | | | | | | | | | | X | | | | | | | | | | X |
| Oregon | X | | | X | X | | X | | | | X | | | | | X | | X | | | X |
| Pennsylvania | | | | X | | | | | | | | | | | | | | | | | X |
| Rhode Island | | | | | | | | | | | | | | | | | | | | | X |
| South Carolina | | | | X | | | | | | | | | | | | | | | | | X |
| South Dakota | X | | | | X | | | | | | X | | | | | X | | X | | | X |
| Tennessee | | | | X | | | | | | | | | | | | | | | | | X |
| Texas | X | | | | | | | | | X | | | | | | | | X | | | X |
| Utah | X | | | X | X | X | | | | X | X | | | | | X | X | X | | | |
| Vermont | | | | X | | | | | | | | | | | | | | | | | X |
| Virginia | | | | X | | | | | | | | | | | | | | | | | X |
| Washington | | | | X | X | | X | | | | X | | | | | X | X | X | | | X |
| West Virginia | | | | X | | | | | | | | | | | | | | | | | X |
| Wisconsin | | | | X | | | | | | | | | | | | | | | | | X |
| Wyoming | X | | | X | X | X | | | | | X | | | | | X | X | X | | | X |

Once you have decided on the species, review the summary information provided in Chapter 6 for each state that offers hunts for your species of choice. Based on that summary, you can request more detailed information for each state and/or get it from the Internet. Many states have information on hunter success rates, hunting pressure, drawing statistics, and other information available to help guide your efforts.

Most states set big game seasons several years in advance. A call or letter now will get you the information needed to schedule vacation, obtain spousal consent, etc. Most states can also send a copy of the previous year's regulations and information on drawing dates for the upcoming year's licenses. Harvest information from prior years should also be obtained. When this information comes in, get together with your group and decide what your approach for the coming year and beyond will be. This is a good time to define long-term strategies and start working on them. Remember that most states limit nonresident licenses and you may need to participate in a drawing.

With this basic information, you're ready to start getting into the details of your trip. Some questions to ask include:

- Are the licenses limited by drawing? When are applications due?
- Will you be hunting public or private land?
- What type of terrain will you be hunting?
- What is the trophy potential of the area and does that really matter?
- What are the expected success rates?
- What type of hunting pressure can be expected?
- What types of amenities/services are available?

Depending on the state(s) and species selected, you may need to contact game biologists and get some more detailed information. Many of them will give you suggestions to help guide your search. Also talk to others who have hunted for that species and solicit their input.

Armed with this information, you're ready to identify areas that meet your criteria. Depending on what you are looking for, there may be only a few or many areas that match what you're looking for. At this point, you'll need to decide what is most important to your group and make your selection. You may want to narrow your list down to two or three areas and get additional information - maps showing public property, topography, etc., to help you decide which is best suited to your needs.

Once you have selected an area, gather as much information as possible. Also try to arrange a scouting trip before the season if it is feasible. If it is not, you might want to arrive a few days early to scout the area. This scouting before the season is particularly useful if the season is short. For a hunt less than 7 days long, scouting before the season is very important - you may not have time to scout and hunt at the same time. Another approach to scouting is to preview areas while driving through on family vacations or business trips. For limited units that may take several years to draw a license, use every opportunity to gather more information. Make notes of what you've learned so you can access the information when you draw.

## Game Distribution

The types of game available and accessible to most hunters in the United States include: deer - Whitetail, Blacktail, and Mule, elk - Roosevelt, Rocky Mountain, and Tule, antelope, bear, caribou, moose, mountain goat, and sheep - Bighorn, Desert, and Dall. Some species are common with unlimited tags available while others have a very limited range with all licenses issued via drawings.

## Drawing Hunts

Drawing hunts represent a variety of opportunities to all hunters and deserve serious consideration and evaluation. Drawings are used by wildlife managers for a wide variety of reasons, including:

- To control the female harvest (important for population control)
- To control hunting pressure and overall harvest
- To distribute licenses where demand exceeds supply
- To permit hunting opportunities at special locations

Each of these reasons presents opportunities. Success rates on female only or either-sex hunts are typically twice that of male-only hunts. By limiting the number of hunters in an area, hunt quality and success are improved and wildlife managers are able to better control the age-structure of wildlife, producing more trophies. Many states offer drawing hunts for species with limited habitat in that state. Due to the limited number of licenses, drawings are the most fair way to distribute them. Drawings are often used to allow access and control hunting pressure on special areas such as military bases, wildlife areas near urban areas, and National Wildlife Refuges.

A lot of hunters do not participate in drawings for a variety of reasons. Some may not be able to plan their trip far enough ahead to commit the license fees when they are due. Others don't understand the process and know that they can always buy an over-the-counter tag and hunt. This is constantly changing as more hunters want access to quality hunts. Hunters that don't participate in drawings are missing some excellent hunting opportunities. Game herds in limited drawing areas generally have a better male/female ratio, better age structure, and may be in easily accessible areas. These hunts are the common man's best opportunity to hunt trophy animals. Many states have developed a preference point system which are designed to ensures that everyone gets the same opportunity at these tags. Every year that you don't draw a license, you get a point which gives you preference in next year's drawing. Remember, regulations vary by state - please check with the wildlife division for specifics.

Remember to do your homework when applying for drawing licenses. Be sure that you will have a productive place to hunt if and when you are drawn. Establish land ownership and access before applying. Most states allow hunters to apply as a group when seeking drawing licenses. Be sure that your hunting companions have the same goals and objectives in mind.

# Estimating Trip Costs

As you develop plans for a hunt, putting together a realistic budget is a good idea. You can use this estimate when talking to others about joining your expedition and be sure that the trip is within your budget. The following guidelines can be used to start your estimate.

**License costs** - These can be obtained from the state that you are planning the hunt in. Be sure that you understand what licenses are required for your trip.

**Guide/Outfitter/Trespass Fees** - Be sure you understand what is included in their fees. Also ask about any "hidden" costs - tips, trophy fees, game retrieval, etc.

**Lodging** - include any costs for camping and hotels/cabins while travelling or hunting. Be sure everyone understands how many people per room while deciding on this.

**Transportation** - Figure the distance to be traveled, the average gas mileage and a conservative assumption for gas prices. If you'll be flying, include airfare, parking, and rental vehicles.

**Food** - For cooking your own meals, figure $6 to $10 per day per person, depending on your tastes. The upper end of this range will provide great food with a little planning! Include meals along the road while traveling to the hunting area. If you'll be dining out, figure $25 to $50 per day per person, depending on location.

**Miscellaneous** - include any special gear that may be required for the hunt, gifts and souvenirs, and anything else not included in the other categories.

Taking the time to estimate your trip costs while in the planning stages will help avoid surprises when the trip actually occurs. You can also avoid disappointment by not going through the effort of planning a trip you can't afford.

## Guided vs Unguided Hunts

Early in the planning process, you need to decide if your hunt will use a guide's services or will be totally do-it-yourself. A lot of factors come into play when making this decision - cost, quality of the hunt, logistics of getting to the hunting area, trophy potential of the hunt, equipment required, regulatory requirements, etc. Reviewing each of these factors can help you reach your decision.

Typically, an unguided hunt will be cheaper than a guided one. However, guided hunts generally have better trophy potential and deserve serious consideration. Some hunters prefer guided hunts so they can focus more on hunting and not have to worry about the logistics and details associated with a do-it-yourself adventure. A guide's services are also valuable when hunting an unfamiliar species or when you get lucky and draw a "once in a lifetime" license. Some states require nonresident hunters to use a guide for hunting in certain areas and/or for certain species.

The cost of a guided hunt can vary widely - from a few hundred dollars to tens of thousands. As the cost varies, so will the level of service and typically the trophy potential.

Outfitters and guides can provide a wide range of services - fully guided hunts, drop camps, trespass hunts and packing services.

A fully guided hunt usually involves the outfitter providing everything except for your personal gear. They provide accommodations, food, and transportation when hunting. A guide typically accompanies one or more hunters or places them on stands each day. The outfitter typically recovers game and can arrange for meat storage, processing and taxidermy.

Drop camps involve an outfitter providing equipment and food (sometimes) for a group of hunters in a hunting area. Transportation to the hunting area is usually provided and may be by horse, ATV, or 4X4. Upon completion of the hunt, the hunters, their gear and any game is brought back from camp.

Trespass hunts involve paying an outfitter or landowner money for permission to access private property. Hunters are typically on their own for finding and recovering game, sleeping accommodations, and cooking.

Packing services are used by hunters to transport them and their equipment into remote areas - usually by horseback or plane. Upon completion of the hunt, the hunter, their gear, and any game taken are brought back to the point of origin.

If you are considering a guided hunt, do some research early on to help determine what the going price is for your hunt. A great place to start is the wildlife agency for the state(s) you are considering. Most states require that guides and outfitters be registered and licensed. Ask for a list of licensed outfitters. You can also get information from local sportsman shows, magazine ads, friends, and the Internet. This basic information will usually consist of a glossy brochure with pictures of hunters and their trophies, some information about where they hunt and the type of services offered, and a price list. Armed with this basic information, you'll be able to decide if a guided hunt is feasible.

Once you've decided that a guided hunt is feasible, prepare a list of questions to ask prospective outfitters. The following list is a good starting point:

- How many days will be spent hunting?
- How many hunters will be in camp?
- How many hunters are in the area?
- What type of food is served?
- What is the trophy potential of the hunting area?
- What is the typical success rate?
- What hunting methods are employed?
- What gear do I need to bring?
- Are there trophy fees for taking a trophy animal?
- Will the hunt be on public or private property?
- How physically demanding is the hunt?
- How many hunters per guide?
- How long have the guides worked for you?
- Is the hunt Fair Chase?
- How will the hunting area be accessed?

Once you've asked your questions and are satisfied that the hunt matches your expectations, ask for references. Be sure to get both successful and unsuccessful hunters. Ask them many of the same questions and the most important one - "Would you hunt with this outfitter again?" Ask the unsuccessful hunters why they didn't take an animal. Avoid any outfitter that won't give references! When calling references, be considerate. Make your calls at an appropriate time - early evening or on the weekend and ask if they have a few minutes to talk about their hunt. Most folks are more than happy to share their experience.

After checking the references, you're ready to commit. Be sure that the outfitter is aware of any special needs or conditions that you may have - dietary, medical, etc. Review the contract carefully, being sure that everything is spelled out - what services are provided, duration of the hunt, fees, etc. Once everything is in order, sign it, pay your deposit, and get ready to hunt!

If you decide on the do-it-yourself route, you'll need to be sure you have the proper gear. The information presented in Chapter 3 will help you decide what equipment is needed for your hunt.

# 3

# Gear

Every hunter worth his or her salt has a small mountain of gear. I've never met a hunter who will admit that they have "enough" gear. When the latest gizmo comes out, nothing short of a 1-800 call or a trip to the local sporting goods store will calm the need. The importance of having the right gear for your hunting trip cannot be overlooked. Your comfort and safety depend on it. Lots of things can go astray on a hunting trip - your gear shouldn't be one of them.

Every hunting situation is slightly different and requires different combinations of gear. This chapter discusses some of the major items fairly common to all hunting camps. Guidelines for selecting and maintaining tents, sleeping bags, and general camp gear are provided. Lists to help keep you from forgetting that crucial item are included.

## Tents

For many hunters, a tent will be home for their big game hunt. It will provide them with shelter and protection from the elements. Just like not having the right clothes and other gear can ruin a hunt, using the wrong tent can make or break a hunt. Tents leaking during rainstorms, collapsing during a blizzard, and being a home to wayward mosquitoes are all memories most of us would rather forget.

There are three basic styles of tents - wall tents, cabin tents and dome tents. Wall tents typically have vertical walls and an internal frame. Cabin tents usually have sloping walls and an external frame. Dome tents generally have sloping sides and shock-corded poles that are inserted into the tent fabric. Tents may be constructed of canvas, nylon, or some new, space-age materials. Material type will affect weight, wind and water resistance, and long-term durability. The framing system has the greatest impact on strength and should be a key consideration when selecting a tent since the strength and stability of your temporary home depends on it.

Unfortunately, there are very few tents ideally suited to all hunting conditions. That wall tent that was so comfortable with the wood stove at an elk camp in the high country may be miserable on an Alabama deer hunt. The old family cabin tent that is great for summer and early fall trips may collapse on you during a November blizzard. Dome tents may not offer enough room for a larger group.

To choose the right tent, the following factors need to be considered:

- Season/Anticipated Weather Conditions - Plan for the worst!
- Access - is weight a consideration?
- Group Size - watch out for and plan for snorers!
- Other considerations - other uses, bugs, snakes, etc.

Understanding potential weather conditions is important to selecting the right tent. High and low temperatures, precipitation, and wind will all impact your decision. Some of the heavier canvas tents are great during colder, windy weather. They will block the wind well and often can be heated with a wood burning stove. Hunting in warmer areas or during early seasons makes lighter nylon tents with windows and better ventilation a better choice. Cabin tents are not particularly good at holding up under a heavy snow load. If you're hunting in snowy country, you can take your chances and maybe wake up when the tent collapses on you in the middle of the night or you can rig a secondary shelter to protect it from heavy snow. Understand how bad the weather can get and choose your tent accordingly!

Access to your hunting area is another consideration when selecting a tent. If you can drive to your camp, weight isn't a primary consideration. If you'll be backpacking into remote areas, lighter is better! Even a few ounces saved here can make a difference. On pack trips, weight also plays a role - even a packhorse can only carry so much.

Your group size should be considered when selecting a tent. Most tents are rated by how many people they can "sleep". Just try packing 4 people and their gear into an 8' by 10' tent - nobody will be happy! Divide the rating by two or three to get a more realistic occupancy rating. I've never heard anyone complain about having too much space in a tent. If your group has light sleepers and/or heavy snorers, consider using several tents for sleeping. Few things are worse than not getting a good night's sleep when hunting. You're tired from hunting all day and the last thing you need it to listen to Joe saw logs all night.

Almost all big game animals rely heavily on their sense of smell to protect them from hunters. A little planning when selecting your accommodations can keep you from stinking like this morning's bacon when you head to the woods. A separate shelter or tent for cooking will reduce odors on you and your hunting clothes. Try to avoid cooking in your sleeping tent if at all possible. We usually use a frame supported carport type of shelter for cooking and eating.

If you are camping in an area with snakes or annoying insects such as black flies or mosquitoes, consider using a tent with a floor and screened door and windows. The old cowboy tale of putting a rope around your bedroll to keep the snakes away worked for John Wayne in the movies, but won't even slow them down in real life.

Before leaving for hunting camp, (and preferably more than 20 minutes before you leave) take a few minutes and be sure your tent is ready. Make sure you have all of the poles and stakes with you. When coming back from a hunting trip, be sure that your tent is completely dry before storing it until next season. Set it up at home and dry it out. Store it in a cool, dry location protected from mice and moths. If you're venturing out with a new tent, set it up at home to make sure you have all the parts and know how to assemble it. If you don't, plan on setting it up in the rain on a dark night - Murphy will find you!

Some pros and cons for tent types and materials:

- Wall tents and dome tents are usually stronger than cabin tents and are better suited to camping where wind or snow may be encountered

- Cabin tents and dome tents usually have built-in floors and screened doors and windows, offering better protection from insects and other vermin.

- Nylon tents tend to be more waterproof although canvas tents can be equally watertight when properly treated.

- Wall tents typically offer the most space but also tend to weigh the most.

What type of tent should you buy? Look at your most likely hunting situations, financial situations, group size, and other potential uses for the tent (like recreational camping with the family). Talk with other hunters about tents and ask what works for them. Then select the tent best suited to your situation. I prefer to bring more tents for a larger group, rather than crowding. We often have a gear tent, used exclusively for storage. This provides dry storage and helps empty vehicles. If you need to make do with with an old family cabin tent consider rigging a shelter over your tent to protect it from snow. It may seem like a lot of work when the sun is shining, but is well worth it when the weather changes. I've often used tarps, ropes and dead trees or lumber to rig a shelter over a tent in snow country. By rigging a ridge pole between two trees or building an A-Frame shelter, you can protect your tent from sudden snow storms.

Personally, I have four tents that work well for my situation. I have three dome tents - a backpacking tent designed for one person, a mid-sized tent capable of housing three hunters comfortably and another larger one that will sleep four hunters and store gear in the center. I also have a 10' by 14' wall tent that is ideal for two or three hunters and can be heated with a wood stove during cold weather. With these tents, I can camp anywhere I can walk, drive, or ride to in relative comfort.

## Sleeping Bags

The importance of a good sleeping bag was indelibly etched in my mind on an October muzzleloader hunt and crappie fishing trip to Kentucky. It was a beautiful fall weekend - highs in the low 60s and lows around 30 - frosty and clear. My sleeping bag was rated for 5 degrees and had a warm flannel lining - perfect, or so I thought. The first night, I thought I was going to freeze to death. My bag had an open top and most of my body heat was escaping through the wide top. By wearing a sweatshirt while I slept, I was able to stay warm and enjoy the rest of the trip, but the lesson learned stuck with me.

Choosing the right sleeping bag or bags is important to enjoying your trip. Today's synthetic fibers and traditional down insulation offer lightweight protection over a wide range of temperatures. A good rule of thumb is to buy a bag rated for 10 to 15 degrees below the lowest temperature you expect on your trips. Depending on the areas and seasons you will be hunting, buying two bags may be a good idea. I have a cold-weather bag rated to 30 below and a warm-weather bag rated to 20 above. This approach provides flexibility and ensures comfort regardless of temperature.

The shape of your sleeping bag is an important consideration. Rectangular bags provide the most space but are notorious for losing heat around your head and shoulders.

Mummy bags are the other extreme, tapered and made to close around the head, minimizing heat loss. Hunters with any hints of claustrophobia will not like this type of bag. Semi-mummy bags can be a good compromise. These bags are tapered although not as severely as mummy bags. They also have a drawstring around the top, allowing you to close the top somewhat around your neck and shoulders.

Look for the following features when buying a new sleeping bag.

- Draft Tubes - these minimize air leaks around the zipper.

- Drawstrings - many of the mummy and semi-mummy bags have one or more drawstrings to adjust the bag around your body.

- Layered construction or stitching to keep the insulation from shifting.

The right sleeping bag will keep you warm but it may not help you sleep. A good cot or sleeping pad is essential to getting a good night's sleep in hunting camp - it will keep you off of the cold, wet ground and keep every small stick from poking you in the back. Your hunting situation determines what will work best for you. A foam or self-inflating pad will do the trick for hunts where weight is a primary consideration. An air mattress or cot can provide more comfort when weight isn't an issue. If your tent has a floor, be careful that the legs do not damage it. My favorite cot is an army surplus field hospital bed. It stands about 28 inches tall, is incredibly comfortable, and allows gear to be stowed beneath it. At nearly 30 pounds, I can only use it when I can drive to camp.

Look for sturdy construction when selecting a cot - some of the lighter models may only last a few trips.

## Picking A Campsite

Campsites, like any other real estate transaction, depend on three things - Location, Location, and Location! Selecting the ideal campsite is an acquired skill and choosing a good site can avoid trouble later. The following list identifies some characteristics of a good campsite.

Campsite Selection Characteristics

**Good Access** - via trail, road, etc. In some cases, poor access may mean better hunting - just be sure you know what you're getting into! Dirt roads can become bogs and steep hills toboggan runs with rain or snow.

**Good drainage** - select a site above any areas that might flood. Before camping along a stream or river, inspect the area for evidence of previous floods. Even small streams can become raging torrents following a thunderstorm.

**Shelter** - a campsite located on a bare ridgetop might have a beautiful view but can turn into a nightmare if the wind picks up. Look for campsites below ridgelines, tucked into pockets of timber.

**Access to hunting areas** - the secret here is to camp close to your hunting area but not too close. I've seen camps pitched right in the middle of a prime hunting spot more times than I care to remember. The noise and scent of your camp may cause the game you hunt to move to another area or become more nocturnal. Better to walk or drive a little more than wonder where the game went.

**Relatively level location** - this eliminates problems like sliding on cots, tables collapsing, etc.

Know and follow the landowner's requirements. Even public land may have restrictions on camping.

Bear populations are increasing across the country and hunters need to take steps to avoid conflicts when hunting or camping in bear country. Keep your camp clean and store food in protected areas away from camp. Some National Forests have special requirements for some areas.

## Survival Gear

Every hunter needs to be prepared for the unexpected - getting lost, getting hurt, getting stranded, making a late kill. Each year, hunters find themselves in situations they never could have even dreamed up. Sometimes, these predicaments are only an embarrassment while others quickly become life threatening. A little planning and some simple gear can turn most potentially dangerous situations into manageable ones.

Two simple things can help avoid catastrophe - communication and a survival kit.

**Communication** - let others know where you will be, what you're driving, how you got there, when you should be back. Even if you'll be hunting in another state, rarely will you be going in blind, unable to tell someone where you'll be. In camp, tell your hunting partners where you're going each day and when to expect you back. If you're hunting solo, leave a note in your camp or vehicle describing your plans. Portable two-way radios are a great idea for hunting parties - check local laws regarding their use when hunting. In many areas, cellular phones can summon help quickly. Be sure you are aware of any medical conditions that others in your group may have.

**Survival Kit** - Many people think survival kits are only needed on wilderness or backcountry hunts. Unfortunately, some of those same folks have found out the hard way how wrong they are. Almost any hunting scenario can develop into a situation where you'll be spending the night outside, alone. Having a survival kit to help deal with this unexpected campout can make a tremendous difference in your likelihood to survive.

A good survival kit should contain equipment to help you deal with medical emergencies, survive in the elements, and signal for help. You'll notice that food and water were not listed - lack of food and water won't become life threatening for at least 24 hours - plenty of time to freeze to death! If confronted with a medial emergency, dealing with it should be your first priority if you can. Some conditions such as a heart attack or broken bones cannot be effectively dealt with in the field. Cuts, bites, and other injuries can be at least temporarily handled in the field with the right supplies and instructions. Taking a first aid course is a great idea for any sportsman.

Protection from the elements is more critical than food or water. If stranded, you'll want to provide some sort of shelter to help conserve body heat in cold weather or keep you from overheating in hot weather. Shelters can range from space blankets to bough shelters to caves, depending on what is available and your mobility. Season and circumstance will dictate what type of shelter is necessary. Keeping dry and protecting yourself from temperature extremes is the goal when considering shelters. The key is to provide shelter while you are able to don't wait until it is totally dark, you're completely exhausted, and shock is setting in. A small fire is usually a good idea - it will help keep you warm in cold weather, will cheer you up considerably, and will help others find you.

Attracting attention to yourself is important when others may be searching for you. Proper signaling can also attract others to you before your party would even begin searching. The standard distress signal is three shots fired together, repeating every five minutes. In some areas, this won't attract attention until after dark. A loud whistle is probably better than firing shots and can be heard much farther than just yelling. A small strobe light is also good for nighttime signaling. Smoke from a fire can be a good signal - just add some wet or green wood or even wet grass to make more smoke.

What makes up your survival kit depends on where and when you will be hunting. The following list will give you some ideas for stocking your own.

Survival Kit Supplies

- Band-Aids
- Aspirin - good for pain relief and potential heart attacks
- Electrical tape - for closing deep cuts
- Gauze
- First aid cream

- Matches - regular and waterproof
- Small lighter
- Small candles
- Whistle
- Flashlight
- Spare batteries for flashlight
- Water purification tablets
- Small strobe light
- Space blanket
- Nylon cord

All of these items will fit into a small case in your pack or mounted on your belt.

These supplies, combined with items normally carried when hunting - knife, water bottle or canteen, etc. should allow you survive at least several days, barring medical complications. Take your survival kit with you every time you leave sight of your vehicle or camp. Check the condition of your survival kit before each hunting season - matches can deteriorate, batteries will lose power, etc. Remember, its your life - don't go hunting without being prepared to spend the night!

## Clothing

They say that clothes make the man - that saying is particularly true for hunters. Proper clothing is essential to enjoying a hunt and may directly impact your success. The wrong type of clothing can just make you miserable (if you're lucky) or make you a statistic. Understanding the conditions that may be encountered on your trip is the key to selecting the proper clothing. Be sure to look at temperature extremes and not the averages. Based on these extremes, you should be able to bring the right clothes and be prepared to deal with changes in the weather.

Using a layered approach is usually better than wearing a single item matched to the temperature. By planning on layering your clothes, you'll be prepared to deal with weather changes during the day when you may be miles from camp.

It's a good idea to take clothes just for wearing in camp if you have the room. Camp clothes can be used when cooking, standing around the campfire, working on the ATV, and other chores that can leave you smelling like the parking lot of a major truckstop. By keeping your hunting clothes away from these odors, you'll decrease your chances of having your scent give your presence away.

To control scent on hunting clothes, wash them in baking soda or use some of the unscented detergents available. I'll hang my hunting clothes out to dry in pine trees or other areas away from unnatural scents. (I get some strange looks from the neighbors but it gives them something to talk about!) I'll typically keep my hunting clothes in a separate plastic bag along with some items to help mask my scent - pine needles, oak leaves, or other local items. By putting them on only when I'm ready to hunt, foreign odors are minimized. If the weather permits, you can hang them outside at hunting camp to freshen them up.

The lists below can be used to help you plan your clothing needs for your hunt.

### All Hunts

- Pants - 1 pair for every two days plus a spare
- Shirts - 1 for every two days plus a spare
- Socks - at least 1 pair per day
- Boots - matched to the terrain and weather plus a spare pair
- Camp shoes
- Camp clothes - several sets for longer trips
- Handkerchiefs
- Rain gear - every time, even if hunting in the desert!

### Cold Weather Hunts

- Long underwear
- Wool or insulated pants
- Coveralls
- Insulated coat - one for hunting and one for general wear
- Insulated gloves
- Stocking hat/ski mask
- Sweat shirts/pants
- Wool socks

### Warm Weather

- Shirts - one per day
- Light pants

When selecting clothes for hunting, be aware of regulations regarding the use of hunter orange as many states have different requirements. Try to avoid brightly colored clothes when hunting - stick with colors that blend in with the conditions as much as possible. Also stick with fabrics that are relatively quiet - that nylon snowsuit may be really warm, but makes a tremendous amount of noise when walking through the woods. If wearing camouflage clothes, again try to match the expected conditions where you'll be hunting. Many of the existing patterns will match most hunting conditions and specialized patterns are available to match almost every imaginable condition.

Boots are a key component of your hunting ensemble. They should be matched to the terrain and conditions you'll be hunting in. Select a sole type and upper that gives you the traction and support you'll need. With all the synthetic materials used to make waterproof boots today, wet feet can be almost entirely eliminated. If you'll be hunting in swamps, hip boots might be needed. Consider snake leggings or snake-proof boots if you'll be hunting in poisonous snake territory. It's better to have the protection and be able to hunt confidently than to be afraid to venture into thick cover for fear of snakes.

A spare pair of boots can be very welcome if you get your primary pair wet. Air them out at night so they are dry in the morning to help prevent blisters. Also be sure that your boots are properly broken in before beginning a hunt - your feet will thank you!

If you'll be hunting in extremely cold weather (what is considered extremely cold varies, depending on what you're used to!), be sure that you are prepared. Cotton fabrics are very comfortable but very poor insulators when wet. Wool is a good choice for cold weather as are some of the synthetics. Consider polypropylene long underwear and socks - they'll wick moisture away from your body, keeping you warmer. Also, watch your exertion level - if you start to sweat, either slow down or take a layer of clothes off. Getting wet is a sure way to get cold!

Be sure to take enough clothes to get through your hunting trip unless you can wash them. I also like to take along a clean set for coming home. I know my family appreciates it when I don't come home smelling like deer or fox urine!

## Miscellaneous Equipment

Depending on the particulars of your hunt, a lot of additional gear may be required. It is not practical to list everything that would be required for all of the various possibilities. Only experience, applied to your particular situation, can help you decide on what you'll need.

Getting to camp with all the proper gear is too important to leave to chance. A list can be used to make sure you have everything you'll need for a comfortable camp. It can also be used to decide who will bring items to share with other members such as tents, stoves, lanterns, etc. Depending on the particulars of your camp - where, when, how long, some items may not be needed. Use this list to develop your own checklist. Use your checklist when gathering items and when packing them to be sure you don't leave something important at home.

- Tent
- Sleeping bag and cot or pad
- Rope and rope tighteners
- Gas or propane stoves and Fuel
- Lanterns, fuel, spare mantles
- Flashlights and spare batteries
- Ax or hatchet
- Wood saw
- Meat saw

- Cooking gear - See Chapter 4
- Table and chairs
- Chain saw, oil, fuel
- Water containers
- Coolers for food and meat
- Clothes
- Knives - 3 or more per person
- Knife sharpening kit
- Gun cleaning kit
- Food and Camp Supplies - See Chapter 4
- Gun, Bow, or Muzzleloader
- Binoculars
- Camera
- First aid kit
- Thermos
- Canteen or water bottle
- Compass
- Backpack, fanny pack and/or day pack
- Shovel
- Tool kit
- Vehicle chains
- Tow strap
- Duct tape
- Bungee cords
- Heater for tent
- Cooking shelter
- Portable solar or propane shower
- Gas cans
- Tarps
- Game retrieval gear - backpack, ATV, game cart, pack horse, drag rope
- Hoist for hanging game
- Plastic bags for storing meat
- Salt for hides or capes
- Fishing gear

# Food

Good food is essential for a happy camp. A good breakfast can get you started and keep you going throughout the day. Few things are more satisfying at the end of a long day of hunting than to sit down to a warm, filling meal. Bad food or not enough food can spoil a hunt and divide an otherwise happy and cohesive group.

I've had the pleasure of experiencing gourmet cooking in elk camp thanks to my good friend Dennis Blair - crab-stuffed chicken, paeja, bouillabaisse, curry chicken soup, shrimp aspic, steak with roasted red pepper sauce, etc. I've also been in deer camps where there wasn't enough food to go around- generally due to poor planning or greedy hunting partners. Given a choice, I'll take the gourmet grub!

Choosing a camp cook or cooks is important. There are several ways to do this, depending on the makeup of your group. Some groups will have a person or two that really enjoys cooking - that makes selecting the camp cook(s) easy. Keep in mind that cooking for a whole camp is a lot of work and help out by peeling potatoes, washing dishes, etc. Other groups may not have any one person that likes to cook. A good approach for this type of groups is to share cooking duties - consider having each person prepare their "specialty" or be responsible for a particular meal or day.

With a little planning, your camp can enjoy great food. If you're lucky enough to have a chef in your group, you're in for a treat. If you don't have one, consider recruiting one for next season - it is the stuff legendary hunting camps are made of!

In this chapter, we'll provide cooking tips to increase the possibilities, discuss menu planning, help determine how much food to buy, and provide some simple recipes that can be made ahead of time or quickly prepared.

## Cooking Tips

There are many things you can do to improve the variety and quality of food you have in hunting camp. Most of the variety comes from proper planning and having a few surprises up your sleeve. Here are some ideas:

**Add baking capabilities** - you can use a small gas grill, oven in the hunting cabin, dutch oven, or oven for your camp stove. This enables you to add biscuits, cakes, and maybe even homemade bread to your menu.

**Bring a grill** - a small gas grill is wonderful for grilling steaks, chops, burgers and can pull double duty as an oven. It works much better than trying to grill over a wood fire.

**Prepare items at home** - soups, roasts, chili, etc. Freeze them in zipper bags in meal size portions and all you have to do is heat them up.

**Take a pressure cooker along** - you can make a tender pot roast quickly, and cook fresh veggies in minutes.

**Buy complete mixes** - the ones that you just add water to. It will reduce the amount of eggs and milk you'll need.

**Plan meals that are easily prepared** - the camp cook probably likes to hunt too!

**Have a plan for every day** - know what is being prepared and be ready for it. Cook perishable items early in the trip.

**Be prepared for success** - some of my favorite hunting camps meals are freshly killed game or freshly caught fish!

## Menu Planning

Good menu planning is as important for hunting camps as it is for a successful dinner party. Every year, I see lots of hunters wandering aimlessly through the last grocery store before hunting camp, wondering what to buy and how much to buy. It's a safe bet that they won't have great meals and will likely not have enough of something. Beans and weenies probably make up the majority of their meals toward the end of the trip.

By planning your meals in advance, you can prepare items ahead of time, buy some items in bulk or on sale, and be sure that you've got enough food. It also reduces "end of the line" shopping that will save you money and time!

The first thing to do when planning your menu is to define the group. You need to know how many people you will be feeding. Ask about any strong likes or dislikes and be aware of food allergies. Be sure that you understand everyone's expectations on food quality, quantity, and costs.

Understand how your party will be hunting. If everyone stays out from O Dark Thirty until O Dark Thirty, figure on sack lunches. If everyone comes back at lunch, you should plan accordingly.

Another consideration is access to hunting camp. If you'll be backpacking in, weight is a serious issue. You'll probably want to use either "ready to eat" food for short trips or freeze dried foods for longer ones. If weight is not an issue, then the sky's the limit!

Once you understand your group's requirements and expectations, you're ready to begin planning your menu. I try to plan the more complex meals for the day(s) before hunting season, when time is not at a premium. I'll also try to bring a meal already prepared for the day of arrival. Getting camp set up is enough of a chore without having to spend a lot of time cooking.

Plan on preparing food with a short shelf life early in the trip. Fresh seafood, ground beef, deli meats, salad greens, and some fruits may not keep for a long trip. Seafood and ground beef can be frozen to extend their useable life.

I have a list of meal ideas for breakfast, lunch and dinner that form the basis for my menu planning - use them to develop your own lists.

## Breakfast Entrees

- Sausage, milk gravy and biscuits, hashbrowns
- Omelets, toast, hashbrowns
- Bacon, Oatmeal or Grits
- Ham, eggs, toast, hashbrowns
- Scrambled eggs with cheese, sausage links, toast
- French toast and sausage
- Bacon, egg and cheese sandwich
- Pancakes and sausage

Mix and match these and you've got enough unique breakfasts for even the longest hunting camp!

## Lunch Entrees

- Chili, hot dogs
- Beef barley soup, grilled ham sandwiches
- Stew, biscuits
- Hamburgers and fried potatoes
- Open faced turkey or beef sandwiches and mashed potatoes
- Leftovers from dinner
- Potato Soup, sandwiches
- Ham and cheese sandwiches - cold or grilled

Add an apple or orange and some crackers or candy to almost any kind of sandwich (or two) and you've got a good sack lunch. You can always add a salad and fruit (canned or fresh) to a lunch in camp.

## Dinner Entrees

- Grilled Steak
- Spaghetti with meat sauce
- Hamburgers
- BBQ pork steaks

- Chicken and wild rice
- Pot roast with potatoes and carrots
- Hamburger Helper
- Ham Steak
- Ham and beans
- Fried or grilled fish
- Bacon wrapped game steaks
- Other small game in season - quail, pheasant, grouse, rabbit, etc.

Start off with a dinner salad and/or some soup, accompany with bread, rolls, or biscuits, and you've got a complete meal! If your group likes wine, choose one that compliments your meal.

I usually try to have surprise dessert or two tucked away - it makes the meal more memorable. You'd be surprised how welcome ice cream or a fresh cake is during a hunt!

For drinks, a good selection is best. Coffee, milk, orange juice, and tomato juice are all staples in my camps. I typically have each person bring their own soda, beer, and any other exotic drinks. That way, nobody can be upset at the choices or the quantity.

## Buying Food

The task of buying food often waits until the last store just before camp. If you've planned ahead and know the choices, this approach may work well. I prefer to buy most items well ahead of hunting season, taking advantage of sales and giving me time to pick up those items that I forgot.

As soon as the group size is finalized and the menus are planned, you're ready to prepare your grocery list. I've broken the list down into non-perishable items, perishable items, and miscellaneous items that you'll need for camp. Lists are provided for each type along with approximate quantities to buy per person per meal (unless otherwise noted).

Non-Perishable Items
(Including items that can be frozen)

- Pancake mix - usually cheaper to buy the 10# bag at a wholesale club. Look for mixes that only require water
- Syrup - 1 gallon will usually cover 10# worth of pancake mix
- Sausage - ½ #
- Bacon - ½ #, also add a pound or two for bacon wrapped game steak.
- Steak - 1 #
- Jelly - 1 large jar per trip
- Peanut butter - 1 large jar per trip
- Crackers - 1/3 sleeve per person per meal with soup or chili
- Canned fruit - 1/3 can per person per meal
- Canned veggies - 1/3 can
- Hamburger - ¾ #
- Salad Dressing - 1/3 bottle per 4 persons per salad
- Soups - 1 cup per person with dinner, 2 cups as lunch
- Spaghetti sauce - 1/3 jar
- Spaghetti - 2 to 3 oz.
- Coffee

## Perishable Items

- Potatoes - ½ to ¾ #
- Orange juice - 8 oz. per person per day
- Tomato Juice - 4 oz. per person per day
- Milk - varies widely - figure 8 to 12 oz. per day per person plus 8 oz for milk gravy
- Butter - whatever recipes require plus ¼ # per person per week
- Ham - 1/3 # per person per breakfast or lunch; ¾ # per person for dinner
- Apples, oranges, bananas, etc. - 1 per person per lunch
- Bread - 4 - 6 slices per person per day
- Canned biscuits - 2 to 4 per person per meal, depending on size - cook some extra - they're great for lunches too!
- Eggs - two per person per meal plus recipe requirements
- Cheese - individually wrapped slices for sandwiches - 1 slice per sandwich
- Cheese - hard (cheddar, Colby, Swiss, etc.) - 1 to 2 oz. per person
- Salad greens - 1 prepared bag per 4 to 6 persons

## Miscellaneous Camp Supplies

- Paper Plates - optional - figure 1 ½ per person per meal
- Paper bowls - optional - figure 1 ½ per person per meal with soup
- Paper towels - ½ roll per day per 4 people
- Dish soap
- Salt and pepper
- Hot sauce
- Aluminum foil
- Cooking oil

- Flour - for gravy and breading meats - 1 # usually does it
- Sugar - brown and/or white - 1 # is plenty
- Sandwich bags
- Trash bags
- Mustard
- Ketchup
- Spices as desired

## Food Safety

Keeping your food safe needs to be a primary concern when hunting. Weather conditions may change and you may not have a refrigerator available. Here are some tips to keep you food safe:

- Keep plenty of ice in coolers and cool foods promptly
- Use dry ice to keep food frozen for use later in your trip
- Watch for the expiration date on perishable items
- Remember that packaged meats will only keep about 7 days after they are opened - buy your ham unsliced and open it in camp.
- Heat foods thoroughly.

If you're not sure about something throw it out. That 's better than making everyone sick.

## Cooking Gear

Having the right equipment is essential to cooking good meals. I've got two boxes of cooking gear that will let me make almost anything. Here's a list of things in my cooking boxes:

- Cast iron skillets - 10"
- Griddle
- Cast iron Dutch oven - 12 inch
- Teflon skillet - 12 inch
- Pressure cooker
- Large capacity coffee pot
- 1, 2, 4, and 6 quart pots with lids
- Strainer for draining noodles
- Plastic bowl set
- Measuring cup
- Silverware
- Tongs
- Slotted spoon
- Aluminum pie plates
- Cake pans
- 12 quart pan for dishes
- Plastic cups
- Coffee cups
- Can opener
- Bottle of dish soap
- SOS pads
- Wooden skewers

I've put my hunting cookware collection together over the years, buying items at garage sales, flea markets, and from items no longer wanted at home. I'd advise everyone to think twice and ask three times before taking your spouse's prize cookware to hunting camp!

There are lots of ways to cook your food in hunting camp - over an open fire - nostalgic and rustic but don't expect gourmet results - to regular stoves in hunting cabins. I typically use traditional camping stoves for hunting camp. I say stoves because cooking for a large group will likely require at least 3 burners, with 4 being even better. Propane camp stoves are also a good option, especially if equipped to use a 20# propane cylinder. A small propane grill completes my cooking gear.

## Recipes

Here are a few of my favorite recipes for hunting camp. Some of the soups are made ahead of time and frozen in zipper bags.

### Potato Soup

1 ham bone or several ham hocks
1 medium onion, diced
4 stalks celery, chopped
2 carrots, peeled and slices
potatoes, washed and chunked, peeling optional
Salt and pepper to taste

In a large pot, boil the ham bone or hocks, onion, and celery until the meat starts to fall off the bone. Remove the meat and bones and let it cool. While the ham is cooling, add the potatoes and carrots. Add enough potatoes until they reach the level of the liquid - you don't want the potatoes covered by more than ½ inch of liquid. Cover and simmer until the potatoes are cooked. While the potatoes cook, cut the ham into small pieces. When the potatoes are done, use a potato masher or small mixer to blend them into the liquid. Add the ham back into the soup and serve with crackers. Be careful adding salt until the soup is done - you'll get some from the ham.

You can vary the size of this recipe by adding more meat and potatoes.

## Beef Barley Soup

1 chuck roast - 3 #
12 oz. pearled barley
6 carrots, peeled and sliced
1 can corn
1 medium onion, diced
4 stalks celery, chopped
1 bay leaf
Salt and pepper to taste

Combine the roast, onion, celery, and bay leaf in a pot. Cover with water and simmer covered for several hours, until the roast is tender. Remove the roast and add the barley, corn, and carrots. Simmer until the barley is cooked. While the barley is cooking, dice the roast into ½-inch chunks and add it back to the soup. Stir the soup often and be sure you add water as needed - the barley absorbs a lot of water! Remove the bay leaf and season with salt and pepper. Serve with crackers and hot sauce.

## Hashbrowns

Butter
Potatoes
Non-stick skillet

Peel and boil the potatoes whole until almost done. You can do this the night before. Cool and shred them using a grater. Melt some butter over low heat in the non-stick skillet - about ½ to 2/3 stick for a 10 or 12 inch skillet. When the butter is melted, place the shredded potatoes in the skillet - about ½ to ¾ of an inch thick. Pat them down and cover. Cook over low heat until golden brown. Flip over onto a plate, season to taste and serve. A 12-inch skillet will serve 4 hunters.

## Sausage Milk Gravy

1 to 2# Sausage
Flour
Milk

Brown the sausage in a skillet or Dutch oven , crumbling it up. When it is done, remove it from the skillet and place it on paper towels to drain, leaving the grease behind. Add some flour to the grease, stirring it in with a spatula. Add enough flour to make a good roux. Get this good and warm - it should be bubbly. Start slowly adding milk, stirring it into the roux until it is well mixed. Keep the heat on medium high as you add milk and stir continuously. If there are lumps, press them out against the skillet bottom. As the mixture heats up, it will start to thicken. When it is close to the desired thickness, add the sausage back into the gravy and remove from the heat - it should thicken somewhat as it stands. If it is too thick, add a little milk and reheat slightly. Serve over biscuits and fried 'taters!

These next two recipes are great for those combination hunts!

## Fried Pheasant or Grouse

Pheasants or grouse - deboned and cut into bit-sized pieces
Flour
Salt and pepper
Butter or shortening

Season the flour with salt and pepper. Dredge the pheasant or grouse pieces in the flour mixture and fry in butter or shortening over medium heat. Cook only until lightly browned - do not overcook! Serve immediately. Makes a great appetizer or main course, depending on the quantity available.

## Grilled Duck Breast

Duck or goose breasts, de-boned and cut into chunks
Bacon
Garlic salt
Wooden skewers

Thread the breast chunks onto the skewers, looping the bacon around each chunk in an "S" pattern. Sprinkle with garlic salt and grill over high heat, turning once or twice, until the bacon is cooked and the breast chunks are medium rare. Makes a great appetizer or main course, depending on the quantity available.

## Easy Chili

1 lb. ground elk, deer, antelope, or moose
1 can Brooks Just for Chili Tomato Sauce
1 can Brooks Just for Chili Diced Tomatoes with Onions
1 can Del Monte Mexican Stewed Tomatoes
1 can pinto or kidney beans
seasonings to taste

Brown meat, adding seasonings to taste (I add garlic salt, pepper, and a small amount of diced onions). Combine cooked meat and remaining ingredients in a pot and simmer for at least 20 to 30 minutes. Serve with crackers, cheese, and hot sauce. This can also be simmered in a crock-pot at camp or work.

## Fried Steak - Morning, Noon or Night!

Game steaks
Flour
Garlic Salt
Pepper
Oil or shortening

Season flour with garlic salt and pepper to taste. Dredge steaks in flour and fry in oil over moderate heat until browned on each side. Use pan drippings to make milk gravy. Serve with mashed or fried potatoes. This makes a great breakfast!

# 5

# Preparation

Physical preparation is critical to hunting success on many hunts and often gets overlooked. To be successful, you need to be able to actively hunt your target species. This may vary from getting off the ATV and climbing into a tower stand to climbing mountains daily. If you've followed my advice, you have selected a hunting area within your physical capabilities. If you are planning a more strenuous hunt, some physical conditioning might be in order.

Before beginning any exercise program, a visit to the doctor is a good idea. You want to be sure there are no conditions that might be aggravated by a new exercise program. Your doctor can also give advice on what might work best for your particular situation.

If you want to improve your physical condition, the best approach is to do aerobic exercises at least three times per week. You can walk, jog, run, ride a bike, use a ski machine, stationary bike or any other method that elevates your heart rate for at least 20 minutes. Doing this for at least several weeks before your hunt will help - the longer and harder you exercise, the better shape you'll be in.

Don't try to push it too hard from the beginning - increase the intensity gradually to avoid injury.

If your hunt will be physically demanding - say a backpack trip for elk or a sheep or mountain goat hunt, you should increase your preparation accordingly. More aerobic exercise and weight lifting will help you get into shape. Understanding the physical requirements of the hunt and honestly assessing your physical condition will help you determine what needs to be done.

There are only two hard parts to getting into shape - starting a program and sticking with it! Develop a plan for getting in shape and stick to it. Set specific goals - not necessarily for speed, distance, or weight at first, but rather for merely exercising. Specific goals can be used once you have made the commitment to getting into shape and are routinely exercising. Involve your family and/or hunting partners in it. Even if they can only provide moral support, it will help keep you motivated. Once you start this process and have been faithful to your program for a month or more, exercising will become second nature.

## Shooting

Another aspect of physical preparation is practicing with your chosen weapon. Whether you hunt with a muzzleloader, bow, shotgun, or rifle, you need to be prepared to make the shot when the opportunity presents itself.

If you haven't been shooting regularly throughout the year, make time to become a better shot before hunting season. Break out the rifle, clean it up, and get started. A few shooting sessions between now and the beginning of the season may make the difference between success and failure.

A good way to get ready to start the shooting season is to thoroughly clean and, inspect your rifle. Clean the bore (hopefully you did that at the end of last season) and wipe the metal surfaces lightly with oil. Check the screws on the scope rings and bases for tightness. Inspect the stock, sling, and swivels. Now is the time to replace any worn parts and/or upgrade them.

Once the inspection is complete, gather some ammo and head to the range. Now is the time to use up your older ammo and also be sure that your rifle is sighted in with the ammo you will use this season. If you don't have enough to practice and hunt with, get some more. If you are thinking of changing ammo, get a fresh supply.

The first thing to do at the range is to be sure your rifle is properly sighted in. Check your rifle's zero using sand bags. There are many different ideas on how a rifle should be sighted in. Two popular practices include zeroing dead on at 100 yards and zeroing three inches high at 100 yards. The choice depends on many factors including the type of terrain and cover you plan to hunt, the caliber of your rifle, and the type of sights used. Fire several three to five shot groups to ensure that your rifle is sighted in. With a scoped rifle, you should be able to achieve groups of less than three inches at 100 yards. Once you are satisfied with the point of impact, you are ready to begin practicing.

I know - you're thinking, "This is practice! What do you mean, START?" I've been hunting deer and elk nearly 25 years, have taken over 30 big game animals and have yet to shoot one from a bench using sandbags. I've shot offhand, standing, kneeling, sitting, prone, and hanging off the side of a tree at animals ranging from five to 350 yards. Shooting practice starts when you attempt to duplicate actual hunting conditions. Check with the range officials beforehand to be sure you are complying with range rules and safe gun handling practices. You should practice shooting from a variety of positions, using whatever is available for a rest. If you have a bipod, practice using it. Sit with your back against a bench and rest your arms on your knees. Use a tree or pole to practice shooting from the standing position. Shoot offhand - it is a very humbling experience! If the range permits it, shoot at targets at a variety of distances and I shoot multiple shots, simulating follow-up shots. The purpose of this type of practice is to become intimately familiar with your rifle, to learn the limitations of you and your rifle and to develop good shooting habits, like using a rest.

A great man once said "A man's got to know his limitations." Truer words were never spoken for big game hunters. Every responsible hunter has a duty to the animals we hunt. That duty is a quick, humane kill. If you're not sure that you can provide that, it is better to pass on the shot. I have found wounded animals days and weeks after they were shot by others. Not only did meat go to waste, but the animals suffered needlessly.

How do you determine your limitations? The same way you get to Carnegie Hall - practice, practice, practice! A good way to determine your limitations is to shoot at a 12" diameter target. When you can no longer put 4 out of 5 shots in that target, you have exceeded you limitations. This range will vary by weapon, shooting position, and individual. My personal limitations are 125 yards offhand, 220 yards standing with a rest, sitting, and kneeling, 300 yards prone and 350 prone with a bipod. As important as knowing your limitations is your ability to accurately estimate the range to your target. Again, practice is important. A variety of rangefinders can take the guesswork out of this. Most scopes can also be used as rangefinders - check the instruction book.

Another way to improve your range estimating skill is to pick out an object, guess the range, and step it off. Do this at a variety of ranges and with different sized objects. You'll be surprised how quickly your margin of error decreases.

## Vehicle Preparation

Hunting trips often involve a lot of driving, sometimes in pretty rugged terrain. Take a little time before your trip to make sure that your vehicle - truck, RV, and/or ATV, is ready for the trip. Preventative maintenance like changing the oil, a grease job, etc. will reduce the likelihood that your vehicle will fail you. Be sure the tires are adequate and the brakes are good. Carrying a toolkit is a good idea - jumper cables, a tire pump, tow strap, tire chains, and a tire plugging kit can help get you out of a difficult situation. If you are going to a new area, understand what the roads are like to avoid unpleasant surprises - like your car can't drive the last 20 miles to where you intended on camping and hunting due to rough, slippery roads. When hunting, stay on roads and trails open to motorized vehicles.

## The Hunt

After months (or maybe years) of planning, everything is set and the hunt is about to begin. Your gear is packed and ready, you're in the best shape of your life, the rifle is tuned in, you're headed to an area teaming with game - nothing can go wrong now, right?

Wrong! While you were packing, Mr. Murphy ( of Murphy's law fame) has been stowing away in your gear and is waiting for the perfect moment to try to ruin your hunt. Have no fear, something will go wrong during your hunt - the weather, gear, hunting companions. Here are some thoughts and ideas to help you enjoy your hunts more:

**Focus on the hunt.** That's why you came here and spent all that time planning this adventure. Forget about work and the rest of the world you left behind.

**Plan for the next day.** Know what you are going to cook. Prepare the coffeepot before going to bed. Be sure your gear and clothes are ready for the next day.

**Don't work too hard.** Hunting can be hard work; don't do things in camp that make more work for yourself. Keep the meals simple and share the work. If someone appears to be dogging off, ask them to pitch in. They might just not want to get in the way.

**Enjoy the company and country.** This is supposed to be fun. Play cards, swap lies, go fishing, whatever - just relax and have fun!

**Take some time off.** Go into town for supper and a beer.

If it's hot, get an ice cream. A shower halfway through a hunting trip is a welcome break too.

**Try something different.** Use a variety of hunting techniques. Don't be afraid to break tradition. Just don't break any laws!

## After The Hunt

You've just completed your annual hunt. The meat is processed and divided, everyone has had that first glorious hot shower and slept in their own bed again. Time to stow the gear and get back to life, right?

Wrong! Immediately after the hunt is the ideal time to plan the next hunt. Discuss next year's plans and come up with a strategy. Identify any drawings you may want to participate in. Talk about what went wrong and right on this hunt. Modify your equipment list to include the things that you forgot this year. Doing these things while they are fresh in your mind is the best way to ensure that they won't get lost in the blur of everyday life.

After the hunt is also the best time to be sure your equipment is ready for the next trip. A little time now will avoid disappointment and frustration next time. Some tips:

- Dry the tent out.
- Wash the sleeping bag if necessary.
- Drain all the fuel from lanterns and stoves
- Repair any damaged equipment
- Clean and resharpen your hunting knives
- Clean your rifle

Remember, for non-hunters, hunting season is a short time in the fall. For the truly enlightened, there are only two seasons - planning season and hunting season!

# Contact Information

The following pages include summary and contact information for each state. Information on season structures, species available for residents and non-residents, drawing license requirements, access to public lands, hunter safety requirements, and other information is provided for each state. This information is current at the time of printing and typically doesn't change dramatically from year to year. Season structures are provided in summary form - i.e. specific dates are not provided as they may vary from year to year. Contact information is also provided for the U.S. Forest Service and Bureau of Land Management.

This information is intended to be a guide to assist in planning hunts and to identify where additional information can be obtained. Readers are advised to obtain more detailed, current information from the sources provided before committing to any hunt or season.

*Alaska, California, Hawaii,*
*Nevada, Oregon, Washington*

The western United States offers hunters more than 15 species of big game to pursue. With vast amounts of public land and various seasons open almost year-round, do-it-yourself hunts can provide great opportunities. No other region offers the variety of species and habitat that this region offers. Conditions and terrain are widely varied - you can hunt Blacktail deer in the rainforests, antelope and desert bighorns in the deserts, elk, moose, mountain goats, Dall sheep, deer, and bear in the mountains and caribou and musk ox on the tundra. Some states pose special challenges - access in Alaska, logistics in Hawaii, drawing the license of choice in California and Nevada. The opportunities and experiences are well worth dealing with these challenges.

Alaska Department of Fish and Game
P.O. Box 25526
Juneau, AK 99802

Telephone: 907-465-4100
Web Page: www.state.ak.us/local/akpages/fish.game/
E-mail: through web page

| Resident | Non-Resident |
|---|---|
| Bear | Bear |
| Bison | Bison |
| Blacktail Deer | Blacktail Deer |
| Caribou | Caribou |
| Dall Sheep | Dall Sheep |
| Elk | Elk |
| Moose | Moose |
| Mountain Goat | Mountain Goat |
| Musk Ox | Musk Ox |

Alaska can be a hunter's paradise or a hunter's nightmare, with a very thin line often separating the two! With species only available in Alaska and northern Canada, hunters often consider an Alaskan hunt the experience of a lifetime. Alaska is divided into 26 Game Management Units and numerous sub-units for game management. Guides are required for nonresidents hunting Dall sheep, brown and grizzly bears, and mountain goats. Licenses are available over the counter or on-line for most species. Licenses for some units and species are only available by drawing - moose, musk ox, elk, sheep, bison, mountain goat, and caribou. Application forms are available on-line and are due in May. In some units and for some species, hunters are restricted to a license every 4 or 5 years. Black bears may be taken using bait, subject to restrictions. Archery and muzzleloader hunters are required to have special bowhunter and muzzleloader hunting education certifications for some hunts. Hunters may take up to five caribou, three bears, and four deer, depending on units. Most other species are limited to one per year.

## Seasons

Alaska has a complex season structure. Seasons are generally held in August and September and most are closed by sometime in October. Some species have no closed seasons in specific units

**Archery** - Archery seasons are typically held earlier than firearms seasons.

**Muzzleloader** - Some special muzzleloader seasons are available - they are typically held throughout the fall.

**Firearms** - Firearms seasons vary by Game Management Unit and species. Spring bear seasons are held from March through June, depending on unit.

## Suggestions

Alaska often seems like a land overflowing with game. In reality, game densities are typically much lower than in the Lower 48. Due to the access constraints and logistics associated with hunting in Alaska, a guide or someone with intimate knowledge of hunting conditions is strongly recommended. For deer, Kodiak Island is loaded with blacktails. South central Alaska offers good hunting for Dall sheep and moose. Caribou and musk ox are typically hunted in the far north. Try the mountains of southeast Alaska for mountain goats.

California Department of Fish & Wildlife
1416 9th Street
Sacramento, CA 95814

Telephone: 916-653-9664
Web Page: www.dfg.ca.gov/hunting
E-mail: Available from web page

| Resident | Non-Resident |
|---|---|
| Antelope | - |
| Bear | Bear |
| Blacktail Deer | Blacktail Deer |
| Desert Bighorn | Desert Bighorn |
| Elk | - |
| Mule Deer | Mule Deer |

California has some of the longest deer seasons in the nation, with seasons starting in July and continuing until January. The State is divided into zones for management purposes. Deer licenses are available via drawing and over the counter, depending on zone. Hunters may harvest one deer in most zones, with some zones allowing an additional buck or antlerless deer. Antelope and elk licenses are distributed via drawing and are restricted to residents only. Residents may receive only one buck antelope license every ten years. Three species of elk are present in California - Roosevelt, Tule, and Rocky Mountain. Only one desert bighorn sheep license may be issued to a nonresident in the random drawing. Bear licenses are unlimited, with an overall annual harvest quota. Dogs may be used to hunt bears. All hunters applying for drawing licenses must have a valid, current California hunting license. Applications are typically due in early June for all premium licenses.

Information on Wildlife Management Areas is available online, with some maps accessible via the web page. Hunters without a previous California hunting license, valid hunter education card from another state or a current, valid hunting license from another state are required to have a Hunter Safety card. Regulations and season information are available on-line. Hunter success, the number of applications for licenses, and the date quotas were reached are available on-line. Access to public property is also summarized by zone. California has vast amounts of public land for hunters in the form of Wildlife Management Areas and National Forests.

## Seasons

**Archery** - Archery deer seasons vary widely by zone. Seasons start as early as July and August with closing dates ranging into October. Archery bear season starts in mid-August and closes in mid-September.

**Muzzleloader** - Muzzleloader seasons for deer start in October, with seasons running into January.

**Firearms** - Firearm deer seasons also vary widely by zone. Some seasons start as early as August, with most units open during all or parts of September, October, and November. Some seasons extend into December. Bear seasons typically open with the general deer season and close when the annual quota is reached or the last Sunday in December - whichever comes first. Elk seasons range from late-August to early December, depending on area and species. Antelope seasons are held from late August through late September. Desert bighorn seasons start in early to mid-December and close in early to mid-February.

## Suggestions

A deer hunt in the Klamath National Forest is a good way to experience California blacktail deer hunting. With good access to public land, hunters can find seclusion and a variety of hunting conditions. The early deer hunts can offer good hunting, but hunters must be prepared to deal with hot temperatures. Scouting is also more critical during this early season as deer will focus on food and water supplies. The elk and antelope hunts are good for hunters fortunate enough to draw a license.

# Hawaii

Hawaii Department of Land & Natural Resources
Division of Forestry and Wildlife
1151 Punchbowl Street
Room 325
Honolulu, HI 96813

Telephone: 808-587-0166
Web Page: www.state.hi.us/dlnr/
E-mail: not available

| Resident | Non-Resident |
|---|---|
| Axis Deer | Axis Deer |
| Blacktail Deer | Blacktail Deer |
| Feral Goat | Feral Goat |
| Feral Sheep | Feral Sheep |
| Mouflon Sheep | Mouflon Sheep |

Big game on Hawaii is managed by unit and island. Species vary from island to island. Hunting seasons, bag limits and hunting methods are set by unit for each island. Most archery and muzzleloader licenses are available over the counter. Almost all firearm licenses are issued via drawing and specific hunting dates are assigned. Dogs may be used for some species in some units. Many seasons are held only on the weekends. Hunter education or a letter of exemption is required for all hunters.

## Seasons

On private property, hunters may take game animals throughout the year with a valid hunting license. The following summary presents the hunting season structure for public lands.

**Archery** - Specific archery seasons are held for all species, with some units open year round for feral sheep and goats. Mouflon sheep archery season is generally held in late July through early August. Axis deer are hunted in late February. Blacktail deer seasons are held in September and October.

**Muzzleloader** - Muzzleloader season for Mouflon sheep are held in August. Feral goat seasons are held from July through September. Blacktail deer muzzleloader seasons are held in September. Axis deer seasons are held in March.

**Firearms** - Year-round firearm seasons are held for feral sheep and goats in some units. Mouflon sheep are hunted from August through October. Blacktail deer are hunted from July through October, depending on unit. Axis deer seasons occur from March through May.

## Suggestions

Hawaii offers good hunting for several species. With a variety of game and seasons open all year for some species, a Hawaiian hunt can be fit into most vacations. The logistics of hunting here and the short seasons for some species make using a guide's services a very good idea for nonresidents. If you want to try a do-it-yourself hunt here, be sure you understand the seasons and unit boundaries, and that you are prepared to deal with an animal if successful.

Nevada Division of Wildlife
1100 Valley Road
Reno, NV 89520

Telephone: 775-688-1500
Web Page: www.state.nv.us/cnr/nvwildlife
E-mail: ndowinfo@govmail.state.nv.us

| Resident | Non-Resident |
|---|---|
| Antelope | Antelope |
| Bighorn Sheep | Bighorn Sheep |
| Desert Bighorn | - |
| Elk | Elk |
| Mountain Goat | - |
| Mule Deer | Mule Deer |

All big game licenses are issued through a computerized drawing process. Applications are available in mid to late March and are due by mid-April. Drawing results and harvest information from previous years is available on-line. Nevada uses a bonus point system for the drawing process - an extra entry into the drawing is awarded for each Bonus Point.

Their web page has detailed information for each species and Game Management unit, including access, land status, terrain, habitat, map sources, weather conditions, and suggested hunting areas. Hunters born in 1960 or after are required to have a Hunter Safety card.

## Seasons

**Archery** - Nevada only offers archery seasons for antelope, elk, and deer. Antelope seasons start as early as late July and continue into September. Elk seasons are held from mid-August through early October. Deer seasons start as early as mid-August and end by late December.

**Muzzleloader** - Deer and elk are the only big game species with special muzzleloader seasons. They start as early as early September and close as late as mid-December.

**Firearms** - Deer seasons start in early October and some run through late December. Elk seasons start in early August and run as late as mid-January. Antelope seasons start as early as late July and continue into September. Bighorn sheep seasons start as early as early September and close by late December. Mountain goat seasons start in late August and end by late October.

## Suggestions

Nevada boasts tremendous amounts of public lands and also some outstanding hunting for those fortunate enough to draw licenses. In 1999, hunters took two bull elk scoring over 400 inches on public land! The deer hunting can also be outstanding. For elk, almost any unit with an open season is a good prospect. For deer, try the Ruby Mountains units. If you like to or want to hunt sheep, be sure to apply to Nevada. They offer some of the best sheep hunting in the United States.

Oregon Department of Fish & Wildlife
P.O. Box 59
Portland, OR 97207

Telephone: 503-872-5268
Web Page: www.dfw.state.or.us/
E-mail: odfw.info@state.or.us

| Resident | Non-Resident |
|---|---|
| Antelope | Antelope |
| Bear | Bear |
| Bighorn Sheep | Bighorn Sheep |
| Blacktail Deer | Blacktail Deer |
| Elk | Elk |
| Mountain Goat | - |
| Mule Deer | Mule Deer |
| Whitetail Deer | Whitetail Deer |

Oregon is divided into specific units for game management. All antelope, spring bear, mountain goat, and bighorn sheep licenses are issued via drawing for specific units. Bear hunters may not use bait or dogs during any bear season. Deer and elk licenses are available for general seasons over the counter and for specific units via drawing. General licenses are only valid for a specific unit or group of units. Spring bear hunting applications are due in early February. Other applications are due in mid-May. Drawing results and the number of applicants for controlled licenses are available on-line. Preference points are used for controlled hunt licenses with 75% of the licenses distributed based on the average preference points for the group and the remaining 25% distributed randomly. Mountain Goat and bighorn sheep licenses are "once in a lifetime".

Hunter education is required for all hunters younger than 18 years of age. A special Youth "First Time" Program is available for resident youth to increase participation and provide additional opportunities. Oregon has 17 special Wildlife Management Areas, National Forests, and Bureau of Land Management properties that provide significant public land hunting opportunities.

Nonresident participation is limited in all controlled hunts, with a maximum of 3% of bear and antelope licenses available to nonresidents. For deer and elk licenses, nonresidents may receive 5% of the available licenses and 5 to 10% of the bighorn sheep licenses. One half of all nonresident licenses are available through outfitters at twice the cost of drawing licenses.

# Seasons

**Archery** - Oregon has archery seasons for deer, antelope, and elk. Archery antelope seasons start in mid-August and run through mid-September with durations ranging from 8 to 28 days. Archery deer seasons range from late August through December. Elk seasons are split between the western half of the state - late August through September - and the eastern half - late November through mid-December.

**Muzzleloader** - Oregon offers controlled muzzleloader hunts for antelope, deer and elk in select units. Antelope seasons are typically seven to nine days in duration and are held from mid-August to mid-September. Deer seasons occur from late September through early December, with the duration varying by unit. Muzzleloader elk seasons start as early as August and extend into February in some units.

**Rifle** - Rifle antelope hunts occur from mid-August through late October, typically with a 9-day duration. General deer seasons occur from late September through early November, with a split season in some units. Controlled rifle hunts typically start at the same time and run through mid-October. Bull elk seasons typically occur as 4 to 7-day hunts in mid to late October, with cow hunts starting as early as August and extending into February in some units. Bear hunts start in early August and extend through November or December, depending on unit. Mountain goat seasons are usually 12 days in durations and occur in mid to late September. Bighorn sheep seasons are held from mid-August through late October, with length varying by unit.

## Suggestions

Oregon offers hunters a lot of opportunities - seasons running from August to February and seven species of big game. Some suggestions include an archery elk hunt in the western half of the state during early September. The Cascade Range offers lots of public access. A hunt for coastal blacktails offers a unique challenge also - the temperate rainforests have thick cover and lots of food for deer, making hunting them a challenge. Bureau of Land Management properties in the southeast corner of the state offer good antelope hunting.

Washington Division of Fish & Wildlife
600 Capital Way North
Olympia, WA 98501

Telephone: 360-902-2200
Web Page: www.wa.gov/wdfw
E-mail: wildthing@dfw.wa.gov

| Resident | Non-Resident |
|---|---|
| Bear | Bear |
| Bighorn Sheep | Bighorn Sheep |
| Blacktail Deer | Blacktail Deer |
| Elk | Elk |
| Mule Deer | Mule Deer |
| Moose | Moose |
| Mountain Goat | Mountain Goat |
| Whitetail Deer | Whitetail Deer |

Washington is divided into specific units for game management. All moose, mountain goat, bighorn sheep licenses are issued via drawing for specific units. General licenses for bull elk, bear, and buck deer are available for many units, with antlerless and some bull/buck licenses for deer and elk available through the drawing process. Washington's drawing process uses a weighted point draw - your odds increase with more points. Drawing information is available on their web page and applications are due by early June. Moose, mountain goat, and bighorn sheep licenses are "Once in a Lifetime". Washington uses a combination license system for big game, allowing hunters to select a combination of animals to hunt. Bears cannot be hunted with dogs or bait.

Hunter education is required for all hunters born after January 1, 1972. Harvest statistics are available on-line. Washington has Wildlife Management Areas throughout the state. Information including size, species present, contact information and maps are available on-line.

## Seasons

**Archery** - Washington offers archery seasons for deer and elk. A split deer season typically runs the month of September, with the second split held from late November through mid-December. The archery elk season is held from early to mid-September with a late season running from late November through mid-December.

**Muzzleloader** - Washington has specific muzzleloader seasons for deer and elk. An early "High" deer season is held from mid-September through late September. An early general season occurs in mid-October and a late season is held from late November through mid-December. The muzzleloader elk season is also held in mid-October, with a late season held from late November through mid-December.

**Firearms** - Three firearms deer seasons are held - the "High" season in mid-September, the general season in mid-October, and a late season in mid-November. Elk seasons are held in late October through early November in the eastern part of the state and early to mid-November in western Washington. Bear seasons start in either early August or early September and typically close in mid to late November. Moose season runs from early October until late November. Mountain goats may be hunted from mid-September through late October. Bighorn sheep are hunted from mid-September until mid-October.

## Suggestions

Washington has strong elk and deer populations. Elk hunting on the east side is for spikes with a general license, with branch antlered bulls by drawing only. Trying to draw one of these licenses and falling back on the general license would be a good strategy. Elk populations are also increasing in Spokane, Stevens, and Ferry Counties. Deer numbers are high in the Spokane area, making this area a good choice for deer hunters. Washington has one of the highest bear populations in the Lower 48. A fall bear hunt centered around food sources is also a good bet.

# Rocky Mountains

Arizona, Colorado, Idaho, Montana,
New Mexico, Utah, Wyoming

Variety is the word for big game hunting in the Rocky Mountain Region. Hunters have opportunities to pursue 12 species of big game animals. States in this region are home to most of the elk, antelope, and mule deer in the United States. Good opportunities for moose, bighorn sheep, desert bighorn sheep, and bison await those hunters lucky enough to draw the license. Black bear numbers are typically increasing through sound management and spring and fall hunts are available. Growing whitetail deer populations and some outstanding trophy potential are making this region more and more of a whitetail deer hunting destination. Public land, in the form of National Forests, Bureau of Land Management lands, and state owned or leased properties, makes access to great hunting a simple matter. A wide variety of terrain is also present - game may be found from above timberline to dense thickets along rivers. Combination big game hunts or big game/small game combinations are a great way to enjoy this beautiful region.

Arizona Game & Fish Department
2221 West Greenway Road
Phoenix, AZ 85023

Telephone: 602-942-3000
Web Page: www.gf.state.az.us/
E-mail: Available through Web Page

| Resident | Non-Resident |
|---|---|
| Antelope | Antelope |
| Bear | Bear |
| Bighorn Sheep | Bighorn Sheep |
| Bison | Bison |
| Desert Bighorn | Desert Bighorn |
| Elk | Elk |
| Mule Deer | Mule Deer |
| Whitetail Deer | Whitetail Deer |

Arizona is divided into specific units for game management. All antelope, elk, bighorn sheep, desert bighorn and bison licenses are issued via drawing for specific units. Applications are typically due in mid-June. Some bear and some deer licenses are available over the counter. A "drawing only" spring bear season is held with applications due in mid-October. Hunters wishing to apply for drawing licenses are required to purchase an Arizona hunting license before applying. Nonresidents are typically allocated 10% of the licenses for bull elk, sheep, and some deer units. Bonus points, which grant another entry into the drawing, are awarded to unsuccessful applicants for elk, antelope, sheep, and buffalo. Ten percent of the available licenses are allocated to the bonus drawing pool. Bighorn sheep, bison, and desert bighorn licenses are "once in a lifetime". Hunter education is required for hunters younger than 14. Regulations and general game distribution maps are available on their webpage.

## Seasons

Arizona's complex season structure is difficult to summarize succinctly. Seasons vary by species and game management unit. Consult the regulations for more details.

**Archery** - Arizona offers archery seasons for elk, deer, bear, and antelope. Elk season is typically held in mid to late September, with some units having seasons in November. Deer archery seasons occur from late August through September, with some season in December and January. Archery bear season is held in mid to late August. The archery season for antelope is typically held in late August through early September.

**Muzzleloader** - Currently, Arizona has muzzleloader seasons for deer and elk. The elk muzzleloader season is held in early or late October, depending on unit. Muzzleloader deer seasons are held in late October or early November, with some held in mid to late December.

**Firearms** - Firearm hunts vary widely by species, unit and sex. Deer seasons occur primarily from late October though late December. Elk seasons are held in early October through early December. Antelope seasons are held in late September or early October. Fall bear seasons are held from late August through either late October or late December. Spring bear seasons begin as early as late March, with some extending into late April. Bison, bighorn sheep, and desert bighorns are typically hunted in either October or December. Rifle seasons are typically short for most species.

## Suggestions

Arizona has excellent public land hunting opportunities for all species. Game Management Unit 9 is a perennial elk trophy elk producer. The Kaibab Plateau offers excellent trophy mule deer hunting and archery tags can be purchased over the counter. Arizona offers more desert bighorn licenses than any other state. Excellent Coues whitetail hunting is also available. Applying for drawing licenses in Arizona requires a financial commitment - non resident hunters must purchase a hunting license before applying. The quality of game found in the state is worth the cost. I suggest applying for several species at a time to improve your drawing odds and to get the most from your hunting license purchase. It may take a few years to draw, but the opportunities are worth it!

# Colorado

Colorado Division of Wildlife
6060 Broadway
Denver, CO 80216

Telephone: 303-279-1192
Web Page: www.dnr.state.co.us/wildlife
E-mail: askdow@state.co.us

| Resident | Non-Resident |
|---|---|
| Antelope | Antelope |
| Bear | Bear |
| Bighorn Sheep | Bighorn Sheep |
| Desert Bighorn | - |
| Elk | Elk |
| Moose | Moose |
| Mountain Goat | Mountain Goat |
| Mule Deer | Mule Deer |
| Whitetail Deer | Whitetail Deer |

Colorado has just implemented a new season structure effective for all game management units west of I-25. There are four big game seasons - the first is "Elk only" and the remaining three are combination deer and elk seasons. All deer, antelope, moose, mountain goat, bighorn sheep, cow elk, and early season bear licenses are issued by drawing. All licenses for the first "Elk only" season are also issued by drawing. All muzzleloader licenses are issued via drawing. Applications are typically due by early April, with results available in June. Bull elk, general season bear, and archery elk licenses may be purchased over the counter for most units. Nonresidents are restricted to no more than 40% of the drawing licenses for deer and elk, with specific limits for other species. Youth licenses are available for hunters under 16 years of age and they can receive preference for doe deer and antelope and cow elk licenses.

Colorado uses a preference point system for allocating big game licenses and annually publishes the results from the previous year's drawing to help hunters understand their chances of drawing a license. A Wildlife Ranching program offers access to private ranches for residents (via drawing). Hunter education is required for hunters born on or after January 1, 1949.

## Seasons

**Archery** - Colorado offers specific archery seasons for deer, elk, bear, antelope, moose, mountain goat, and bighorn sheep. The general archery elk and deer season for units west of I-25 is held from late August through late September. East of I-25, there are three split archery deer seasons - one in October, one in November and the third in

December. Antelope season is held from mid-August through late September. Bear and moose seasons are held from early through late September. Mountain goats and bighorn sheep seasons are held from August through October, with starting dates and durations varying by unit.

**Muzzleloader** - Special muzzleloader seasons are held for deer, elk, bear, moose and antelope. West of I-25, deer, elk, moose, and bear seasons are held in mid-September. East of I-25, deer seasons are typically held in mid-October. Antelope seasons are held in late October.

**Firearms** - Colorado has four rifle seasons for units west of I-25. The first, held in mid-October is only for elk and bear. The second and third seasons are for deer, elk, and bear and are held in late October and early November, respectively. The fourth season is for elk, bear, and deer (only in select units), and occurs in mid-November. Special deer and elk seasons on private land start as early as September and extend though January in some units. East of I-25, two deer season are held in most units - one in late October through early November and a late season in early to mid-December. Moose season is held in early October. Mountain goat, bighorn sheep, and desert bighorn are hunted from August through January, with start dates and durations varying by unit.

## Suggestions

Colorado has the largest elk herd in North America and several areas - units 1, 2, 10, 61, and 201, are managed for trophy bulls. These licenses are issued by drawing and it may take several years to draw. A good strategy is to apply for a bull license as a first choice and a cow license as a second choice. If you draw the cow license, use the hunt as an opportunity to scout the area for your future bull hunt. Colorado also offers archery and muzzleloader elk seasons during the rut. This is a great opportunity to get away from some of the crowds and enjoy the beautiful fall weather. Colorado's September bear season is also gaining popularity as bear populations increase. The licenses are issued by drawing. The southwestern portion of the state has the highest bear densities, exceeding 1 per square mile in some areas. Hunters wanting to take bighorn sheep, moose, and mountain goat should start applying - it takes at least three years to be in the drawing.

Idaho Department of Fish & Game
P.O. Box 25
Boise, ID 83707

Telephone: 1-800-635-7820
Web Page: www.state.id.us/fishgame/
E-mail: idfginfo@idfg.state.id.us

| Resident | Non-Resident |
|---|---|
| Antelope | Antelope |
| Bear | Bear |
| Bighorn Sheep | Bighorn Sheep |
| Elk | Elk |
| Moose | - |
| Mountain Goat | Mountain Goat |
| Mule Deer | Mule Deer |
| Whitetail Deer | Whitetail Deer |

Idaho offers significant opportunities for residents and non-residents for deer, elk, and bear. With nearly 70% of the state in public ownership, hunters can find access in most areas. The number of non-resident hunters for deer and elk is controlled by a quota system with general season tags sold on a first come/first serve basis. Tags generally go on sale in December for the following year. Nonresident participation in controlled hunts is limited to 10% of the available licenses.

Idaho also offers spring and fall bear hunting, with baiting and hounds permitted in some units. Moose can only be hunted by residents or former residents who purchased a lifetime license. Residents and non-residents can hunt Rocky Mountain Bighorns, California Bighorns, and mountain goats. There is a two-year waiting period for those successful in drawing a license for moose, sheep, and mountain goats. Hunters who take these species are restricted from further drawings. Persons who apply for bighorn sheep or mountain goats cannot participate in other controlled hunts drawings for that calendar year. Special controlled hunt application dates vary - January/February for spring bear, April for moose, bighorn sheep and mountain goats, and May for elk, deer, and antelope.

Idaho's website has a tremendous amount of information available - from drawing odds and harvest statistics, to information on State Wildlife Areas to on-line applications and license purchasing.

## Seasons

**Archery** - Idaho has specific archery seasons for deer, elk and antelope. Deer seasons typically start in late August and extend into late September, with some late seasons in December. Elk season is held during the same time frame in most units, again with some late hunts in December. Archery antelope seasons generally start in mid-August.

**Muzzleloader** - Only deer and elk have specific muzzle-loader seasons in select units, with deer seasons in October, November, and December. Elk hunters have more muzzleloading opportunities, with lots of November seasons and some December hunts.

**Firearms** - Many of the deer and elk firearms seasons are concurrent and are typically held in early to late October. Some deer seasons occur in November and December, with the later hunts being focused more on whitetail deer. Antelope seasons are typically held in late September through late October. Moose and mountain goats are generally hunted from late August through late November. Bighorn sheep seasons open in either late August or early to mid-September and close in mid to late October. Spring bear season are held from mid-April through either mid or late May. Fall bear seasons open from late August through mid September and close in late October or November.

## Suggestions

Idaho recently revised their season structure to provide more opportunities for hunters to pursue deer and elk on the same trip. They also have two types of elk tags - A &

B, each with different seasons and restrictions. Spike elk are the only legal game in some units with Type A tags. Idaho's whitetail deer population is increasing with excellent trophy potential and some special seasons to take advantage of this. Idaho also has a strong moose population. Resident hunters should apply for a moose license.

# Montana

Montana Fish, Wildlife, and Parks
1420 East 6th Avenue
Helena, MT 59620

Telephone: 406-444-2535
Web Page: www.fwp.state.mt.us/
E-mail: Available through Web Page

| Resident | Non-Resident |
|---|---|
| Antelope | Antelope |
| Bear | Bear |
| Bighorn Sheep | Bighorn Sheep |
| Elk | Elk |
| Moose | Moose |
| Mountain Goat | Mountain Goat |
| Mule Deer | Mule Deer |
| Whitetail Deer | Whitetail Deer |

Montana is divided in districts for game management. District boundaries are available via the web page. All moose and mountain goat licenses and most antelope and bighorn sheep licenses are issued via drawing for specific units. Nonresident participation is limited in almost all hunts to a specific quota or 10% of the available licenses. Nonresidents must first draw a deer or elk license before applying for special hunts. An unlimited number of antelope licenses and bighorn sheep licenses are available for a few units. Nonresident applications are typically due in mid-March. Resident license applications are due at different times from April through September, depending on species. Information regarding competition for licenses is available on the web page and drawing results may be accessed on-line. Hunter education is required for hunters between the ages of 12 and 17 and bowhunter education is required for all archery hunters. Regulations are available on the webpage.

Montana has a tremendous amount of public land in national forests and BLM land. The also have a Block Management Program that provides access to 7.5 million acres of private property on 900 ranches throughout the state. Descriptions and contact information are available on the webpage. Reservations are available for these properties and hunter pressure is controlled to ensure a quality hunting experience.

## Seasons

**Archery** - Montana offers archery seasons for elk, deer, and antelope. Elk and deer seasons are concurrent in most districts and are typically held from early September through mid-October. The archery season for antelope is typically held from early September through early October.

**Muzzleloader** - Currently, Montana does not have a special muzzleloader season for any species. Some districts have weapons restrictions limiting hunters to muzzleloaders and other short-range weapons for deer and elk.

**Firearms** - Montana has one of the longest firearm seasons in this region for elk and deer - typically five weeks starting in late October and running through late November. Some backcountry areas have earlier starting dates - usually the middle of September. Antelope seasons start in early October and run through early November. Fall bear seasons are held from mid-September through late November. Spring bear seasons are held from mid-April through mid-May. Moose, bighorn sheep, and mountain goats are typically hunted in from early September through late November.

## Suggestions

Montana has a five-week general elk and deer season, offering hunters lots of opportunities to hunt a variety of conditions and wait for weather to start the migration, if they choose. A good strategy would be to apply for a license and if drawn, apply for a special permit for a late hunt outside of Yellowstone National Park. This hunt offers excellent trophy potential for bull elk migrating out of the park. If you elect to hunt the general season, waiting until later in the season when some snow has fallen is a good strategy. Montana is also a trophy whitetail deer destination, with the Milk River area being among the best areas to hunt. Hunters can usually purchase an additional antlerless whitetail deer license if they choose to. Montana is the only state offering unlimited bighorn sheep licenses in a few districts. Hunters should understand that quotas are used to control the harvest in these areas, with the season closing after the quota is reached. Hunter competition can be significant and the season may close after only a few days. The eastern plains offer great antelope hunting with good access to public lands and private property through the Block Management Program.

New Mexico Game & Fish Department
P.O. Box 25112
Santa Fe, NM 87504

Telephone: 505-827-7911
Web Page: www.gmfsh.state.nm.us/
E-mail: Available through Web Page

| Resident | Non-Resident |
|---|---|
| Antelope | Antelope |
| Barbary Sheep | Barbary Sheep |
| Bear | Bear |
| Bighorn Sheep | Bighorn Sheep |
| Desert Bighorn | Desert Bighorn |
| Elk | Elk |
| Ibex | Ibex |
| Mule Deer | Mule Deer |
| Oryx | Oryx |

New Mexico is divided into specific units and regions for game management. Unit designations vary by species. All antelope, elk, bighorn sheep, oryx, desert bighorn, and Ibex licenses are issued via drawing for specific units. Bear, Barbary Sheep, and some deer licenses are available over the counter. Dogs are allowed for bear hunting. Licenses for deer and elk have three designations - Standard, Quality, and High Demand. Residents pay the same for each designation, while nonresidents pay premium prices for Quality and High Demand licenses. Nonresidents are allocated 22% of the licenses for almost all units and species, The annual big-game proclamation is usually out in March with license applications due in late April. Drawing results are available via telephone or the Internet. Bighorn sheep and desert bighorn licenses, as well as well as a few elk licenses are "once in a lifetime". Hunter education is required for hunters younger than 18 and for all hunters in specific units - primarily military bases.

## Seasons

**Archery** - New Mexico has archery seasons for deer, elk, and antelope. Deer seasons typically start in early September and close in late September. Some areas have late seasons from early to mid-January. Elk seasons are also held in September, opening in early to mid-September and closing in mid to late September. Archery antelope season is held in mid August.

**Muzzleloader** - Special muzzleloader hunts are held for deer, elk and antelope. Deer seasons occur in late September and early October. The majority of elk seasons are held in October, with some in November and

December. Antelope muzzleloader hunts occur in August and September.

**Firearms** - Most firearm deer seasons are held from late October through mid-November. Elk firearm seasons typically open in late September and October, with some units having hunts in November, December, and January. Antelope seasons are typically held from late August through early October. Ibex are generally hunted from September through February, depending on unit. Bighorn sheep seasons are held from September through January. Barbary Sheep are hunted in either early to mid-November or mid-January through mid-February. Fall bear seasons start in early October and close in mid-December.

## Suggestions

New Mexico has some of the best public land hunting opportunities for elk although drawing a license can take time. I recommend applying for the Quality hunts for deer and elk. The hunts on Valle Vidal are probably the best public land hunts in America and you'll face long odds to draw - the results should be worth the wait! New Mexico also is the only state to offer hunts for free-ranging Ibex, Oryx, and Barbary sheep. New Mexico is also a good destination for sheep hunters offering licenses for bighorns and desert bighorns. The licenses are expensive and the drawing odds slim, but milder weather produces trophies every year!

Utah Division of Wildlife Resources
Box 146301
Salt Lake City, UT 84114

Telephone: 801-538-4700
Web Page: www.nr.state.ut.us/dwr/dwr.htm
E-mail: nrdwr.sfowlks@state.ut.us

| Resident | Non-Resident |
|---|---|
| Antelope | Antelope |
| Bear | Bear |
| Bighorn Sheep | - |
| Bison | Bison |
| Desert Bighorn | Desert Bighorn |
| Elk | Elk |
| Moose | Moose |
| Mountain Goat | Mountain Goat |
| Mule Deer | Mule Deer |

Utah is divided into specific units for game management, with some deer and elk licenses available over the counter. All moose, mountain goat, bighorn sheep, desert bighorn sheep, antelope, bear, and bison licenses, as well as many deer and elk licenses are issued via drawing for specific units. Moose, mountain goat, bighorn sheep, desert bighorn sheep, and bison licenses are "once in a lifetime", and waiting periods ranging from two to five years apply to some deer, bear, elk and antelope licenses. Application dates vary, depending on species and license type, with the first applications due in late January. A second application period occurs in May. Drawing results and statistics are available on-line. Utah uses a "Bonus Point" system to assist with license drawings. Approximately 50% of the limited entry licenses are distributed based on bonus points and the rest are allocated randomly.

Hunters may use dogs and bait, subject to restrictions, when hunting bear. Hunter Safety is required for all hunters born after December 31, 1965.

## Seasons

**Archery** - Utah offers specific archery seasons for deer, antelope, elk, and bear. Most archery seasons start in mid to late August and extend into early September (October for bears). Some units have extended archery seasons for deer and elk.

**Muzzleloader** - Currently Utah only offers specific muzzleloader seasons deer and elk. Muzzleloaders may be used during firearm seasons. The deer season starts in late September and ends in early October. Elk muzzleloader season starts in early November and runs through mid-November.

**Rifle** - Rifle deer hunts occur primarily in late October, with elk hunts occurring in early October. Antelope seasons start in early September and run through late September. Moose season is split, with a September segment and an October segment. Antlerless hunts for these species are typically longer and may extend later in the year. Bear may be hunted from late August through early October and again through November. Desert bighorn sheep season is held from late September through mid-November. Rocky Mountain bighorn sheep seasons start in either late September or early November and run through late November. Bison are found in two areas and are hunted in November or December, depending on unit.

## Suggestions

Utah has a Cooperative Wildlife Management Program which allows resident hunters access to 1.2 million acres of private land via special drawing. This program provides excellent trophy potential. Nonresidents may buy licenses from landowners participating in this program. More than 60% of the state is publicly owned and provides good opportunities for big game hunters. Bowhunters might try hunting one of the extended archery seasons for deer and/or elk.

The Uinta Mountains in the northeast part of the state offer good elk and deer hunting. Access to public lands is good with two National Forests providing plenty of space. Some of the National Forests in the southwestern part of the state also offer good mule deer hunting. Some of the smaller tracts of the Wasatch National Forest can provide good opportunities as well. Make sure you know where you're hunting and respect private property.

Wyoming Game & Fish Department
5400 Bishop Blvd.
Cheyenne, WY 82006

Telephone: 307-777-4600
Web Page: gf.state.wy.us/
E-mail: Through Web Page

| Resident | Non-Resident |
| --- | --- |
| Antelope | Antelope |
| Bear | Bear |
| Bighorn Sheep | Bighorn Sheep |
| Bison | - |
| Elk | Elk |
| Moose | Moose |
| Mountain Goat | Mountain Goat |
| Mule Deer | Mule Deer |
| Whitetail Deer | Whitetail Deer |

Wyoming is divided into specific units and regions for game management All antelope, moose, mountain goat, bighorn sheep, and bison licenses are issued via drawing for specific units. Almost all antelope licenses are for any antelope. Some regions have general licenses for bull elk and buck deer, with some regions offering either-sex licenses for deer. General licenses are only valid for a specific unit or group of units. Many units have limited quotas for elk. Most antlerless licenses are issued via drawing, with reduced cost licenses available in some units. Drawing information is usually available in late December with elk applications due by the end of January. Other applications are due from late February to mid March. Results are available via 900 number. Successful applicants for moose and bighorn sheep must wait five years before applying again - preference points are used for these species. Mountain goat licenses are "once in a lifetime". Youth licenses are available for residents and non-residents.

## Seasons

**Archery** - Wyoming has specific archery seasons for deer, elk, moose, bear, bighorn sheep, mountain goats, and antelope. Deer, elk, and moose seasons typically start in early September and close in mid to late September. Bighorn sheep, bear antelope, and mountain goat seasons typically start in early to mid-august and close in mid to late August. Spring bear archery season is held from mid to late April.

**Muzzleloader** - Currently Wyoming only offers muzzleloader seasons for antelope in a few units. Muzzleloaders may be used during firearms seasons. The available seasons start in mid-August and early September.

**Firearms -** Many of the deer seasons are held in October and November, with some opening as early as September and extending into December. Elk firearms seasons typically open in September and October and close in October, November, and December, depending on unit. Antelope seasons are typically held from September through late October. Moose are generally hunted from early to mid-September. Bighorn sheep seasons are held from mid-August through late October. Mountain goat seasons are held from early September through late October. Spring bear seasons are held from early May through mid to late June. Fall bear seasons start in either September or October and close in late September or late October.

## Suggestions

Wyoming has the largest antelope herd in North America. By limiting the number of licenses, success rates on all species are generally above nationwide averages. Nearly ½ of the state is publicly owned and provides excellent opportunities for do-it-yourself hunts. Non-residents are required to have guides in designated wilderness areas. Wyoming also offers good upland game hunting and great fishing. Some of the late seasons offer excellent trophy elk hunts for units surrounding Yellowstone National Park.

Illinois, Indiana, Iowa, Kansas, Michigan, Minnesota, Missouri, Nebraska, North Dakota, Ohio, Oklahoma, South Dakota, Texas, Wisconsin

Deer, especially big whitetails, are the primary species for this part of the country. All states in this region offer excellent trophy potential and most offer hunters the opportunity to harvest additional antlerless deer. Mule deer are found in some of the western plains states in this region. Bear are found in northern portions of this region. Moose, elk and antelope opportunities are limited, but an outstanding potential for success awaits those who draw a license. Public hunting land availability varies widely from state to state. Combination hunts for big game and upland game/waterfowl are ideal ways to enjoy this diverse region of the country.

# Illinois

Illinois Department of Natural Resources
524 S. Second Street
Springfield, IL 62701

Telephone: 217-782-6834
Web Page: http://dnr.state.il.us/
E-mail: Available through Web Page

| Resident | Non-Resident |
| --- | --- |
| Whitetail Deer | Whitetail Deer |

Deer seasons in Illinois are set state-wide, with permit numbers established by county. Archery licenses are available over the counter for residents and nonresidents. All firearms and muzzleloader licenses are issued via drawing, with applications typically due in late April. Hunters may only take one antlered deer per year via all methods. Either-sex and antlerless only licenses are available. License numbers and harvest statistics are available online. Hunter safety or proof of previous hunting license is required for all hunters born on or after January 1, 1980. Information on Conservation Areas is available on their web page and includes contacts, size, habitat, species present and directions.

## Seasons

**Archery** - Archery season typically starts October 1st and extends until mid - January. Archery season is closed during the firearms season in most counties.

**Muzzleloader** - Illinois has a 3-day muzzleloader season in early December.

**Firearms** - Firearms season for deer consists of two seasons - a 3-day hunt in mid-November and a 4-day hunt in early December. Some counties have a 3-day antlerless-only pistol season during mid-January.

## Suggestions

Illinois is famous for big whitetails! Pike County is a traditional hotspot but has very limited public property available. Most of the private property is leased so getting access may be difficult. Other areas in northern Illinois have good deer populations and aren't quite as popular - just be sure you have a place to hunt before applying for the license. The Mississippi river bottoms offer thick cover and hold some deer. Another good possibility is southern Illinois. With the Shawnee National Forest, access to good hunting is much easier to obtain. Southern Illinois also offers great goose hunting, opening great combination hunt possibilities around Carbondale or Marion.

Indiana Division of Fish and Wildlife
402 W. Washington Street, Room W273
Indianapolis, IN 46204

Telephone: 317-232-4080
Web Page: www.state.in.us/dnr/
E-mail: Not Available

| Resident | Non-Resident |
| --- | --- |
| Whitetail Deer | Whitetail Deer |

Deer licenses are available over the counter or may be bought through the mail. Whitetail deer are found statewide. Hunters hunting in Urban Deer Zones may harvest 2 additional antlerless deer. Bonus antlerless licenses are controlled by county and hunters may purchase up to 4 additional licenses. Hunters born after December 31, 1986 are required to have a Hunter Safety card. Regulations are available on-line. Indiana has numerous state and federal properties for hunters without access to private property.

Their web page allows hunters to access this information and includes tract size, species present, contact information, etc.

## Seasons

**Archery** - Indiana has two archery seasons. The early season starts in early October and runs through early December. The late season starts in mid-December and runs through early January. Crossbows may be used during the late season to harvest antlerless deer.

**Muzzleloader** - The muzzleloader season for deer is held from early through late December.

**Firearms** - Firearms deer season is typically held in mid to late November and runs for about two weeks. Only shotguns and handguns may be used to hunt deer in Indiana.

## Suggestions

Indiana has good trophy potential, especially in agricultural areas. Many of the public areas border prime feeding areas and provide cover after the crops are harvested. I suggest hunting on some of the larger tracts - Hoosier National Forest or other larger tracts. Be willing to go beyond where other hunters are willing to walk and your chances improve dramatically. Also hunting later in the season will help you avoid the crowds. You can also contact other landowners in prime-looking areas - it never hurts to ask! Waiting until after opening weekend and/or hunting during the week will reduce crowding as well.

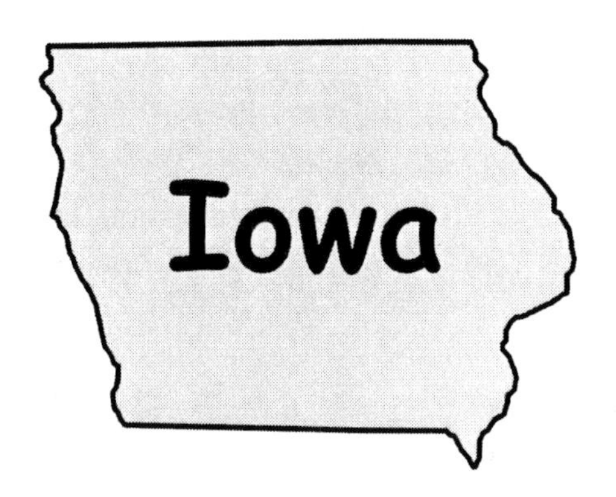


Iowa Department of Natural Resources - Fish and Wildlife Division
Henry A. Wallace Building
900 East Grand
Des Moines, IA 50319

Telephone : 515-281-4687
Web page : www.state.ia.us/dnr/fwdiv.htm
E-mail : Not Available

| Resident | Non-Resident |
| --- | --- |
| Whitetail Deer | Whitetail Deer |

Iowa offers outstanding whitetail deer hunting on both private and public property. An annual quota limits nonresident deer hunters. Phone applications are available for nonresidents and credit cards are accepted. There are two application periods for nonresident deer licenses - one from mid-May through mid-June and a second from late June until late September. The second application period is only for licenses not issued during the first period. Iowa regulations restrict hunters to shotguns only during the firearms seasons.

Iowa has 340 public areas offering more than 270,000 acres for public use. Special regulations may apply. Their web page allows hunters to search for public areas by county and contains information on size, habitat, species present, and location.

## Seasons

**Archery** - Archery season runs from early October until early December and resumes in late December, continuing until mid-January

**Muzzleloader** - There is an early season for residents only - typically 8 days in early to mid-October. The late muzzleloader season starts in late December and continues until early January.

**Firearms** - Hunters may only hunt one firearms season - the early season is five days in early December and the second is eight days is mid-December.

## Suggestions

Iowa offers wonderful possibilities for a combination deer and upland game hunt. With growing deer populations and great hunting for pheasants and rabbits, hunters can combine a trip for both. Look for heavier cover for both deer and upland game - woodlots, thick fencerows, shelterbelts, standing corn, creek and river bottoms. Almost any area of the state is good, but the amount of cover varies widely. The southern part of the state has larger stands of timber that will be more familiar to some hunters. Don't overlook some of the smaller drainages in the eastern part of the state either. I've also jumped some huge whitetails from grass or cattail patch miles from a woodlot when hunting for pheasants in the northeast part of the state. Deer drives are a common hunting method when hunting these smaller patches of cover - be prepared to adjust your methods to meet the situation.

Kansas Department of Wildlife and Parks
900 SW Jackson Street, Suite 502
Topeka, KS 66612

Telephone: 785-296-2281
Web Page: www.kdwp.state.ks.us/
E-mail: Feedback@wp.state.ks.us

| Resident | Non-Resident |
|---|---|
| Antelope | - |
| Elk | - |
| Mule Deer | Mule Deer |
| Whitetail Deer | Whitetail Deer |

All deer, elk and antelope licenses are issued through a computerized drawing process. Whitetail deer are found statewide with antelope and mule deer most common in the western half of the state. Elk are only found on Fort Riley and surrounding private lands. Applications for deer licenses are due by mid-July. Elk license applications are due by the end of July and antelope license applications are due in mid-June. Hunters born on or after July 1, 1957 are required to have a Hunter Safety card. Regulations are available on-line. Kansas has a great walk-in program that allows hunters foot access to private property. Their web page allows hunters to access this database by county and includes maps, tract size, species present, etc. Other State and Federal properties are also listed.

## Seasons

**Archery** - Archery seasons for deer occur in October and November and the second half of December. Archery antelope season is held in late September.

**Muzzleloader** - There are two muzzleloader seasons for deer - one held in mid to late September and the second in mid to late December.

**Firearms** - Firearms deer season is typically held in early December and runs for 12 days. Some units have an extended season in January for antlerless whitetail deer. Antelope season is usually 4 days in early October. Elk season consists of three antlerless seasons - each two months long from September through February and an any-elk season that extends from September through February.

## Suggestions

Kansas is a premier destination for trophy Whitetails! The walk-in program allows access to private property, making it an excellent opportunity! I recommend scouting some of these properties while upland game hunting and applying for a deer license the following year for that unit. It's best to have a backup location too - other deer hunters may have eyes on the same property. You can also contact other landowners in the vicinity during the upland hunting trip - it never hurts to ask! If you're a resident, you should always apply for the elk hunt on Fort Riley - there are some big bulls running around there!

# Michigan

Michigan Department of Natural Resources - Wildlife Division
P.O. Box 30444
Lansing, MI 48909

Telephone: 517-373-1263
Web Page: www.dnr.state.mi.us/
E-mail: Available through webpage

| Resident | Non-Resident |
|---|---|
| Bear | Bear |
| Elk | - |
| Whitetail Deer | Whitetail Deer |

Deer licenses are available over the counter. Bear, antlerless deer, and elk licenses are distributed by drawing, with applications due in mid-May for bear, mid-July for elk, and early August for antlerless deer. Drawing results and harvest information are available on-line. Preference points are used for bear licenses. Hunters may harvest up to two deer per year - additional antlerless deer may be taken depending on area and permits. Baiting is permitted in most areas, subject to restrictions. Dogs and bait may be used to hunt bear in some areas. Regulations and season information are available on-line. Michigan has more than 80 Wildlife Management Areas and four National Forests for hunters without access to private property. Contact information for the Wildlife Management Areas are available on the web page, with maps available on-line for most areas. Special regulations may apply at Wildlife Management Areas. Hunter safety is required for everyone born on or after January 1, 1960.

## Seasons

**Archery** - Michigan's archery deer season consists of an early segment from early October through mid-November and a late segment starting in early December and running through early January. Either sex of deer may be taken.

**Muzzleloader** - Muzzleloader deer season is typically in early to mid December and varies slightly by Zone.

**Firearms** - Firearms deer season typically starts in mid-November and extends through late November. A late antlerless-only season is held in some areas from mid-December through early January. Bear season starts in mid-September and runs through late October. Baiting and dogs seasons vary based on zone. Elk may be hunted during an early split season in late August and mid-September or late during early December.

## Suggestions

Deer hunting is excellent in almost all areas of the state. The Upper Peninsula offers a remote setting and good public access in the Hiawatha and Ottawa National Forests. The archery season provides good opportunities for hunting pre-rut whitetails. Bear hunting over bait or with dogs also provides an early season adventure. Residents interested in elk hunting should participate in the drawing - it's a lot closer than Colorado and the bulls are just as nice. Since youths under 17 may buy a resident license, Michigan is a great place to take a younger hunters on their first out-of-state adventure.

Minnesota Department of Natural Resources
500 Lafayette Road
St. Paul, MN 55155

Telephone: 651-296-6157
Web Page: www.dnr.state.mn.us/
E-mail: info@dnr.state.mn.us

| Resident | Non-Resident |
|---|---|
| Bear | Bear |
| Elk | - |
| Moose | - |
| Whitetail Deer | Whitetail Deer |

Whitetail deer and bear are found statewide. Most deer licenses are available over the counter. Anterless deer and special area permits are distributed by drawing. Bear licenses in the northeast portion of the state are also issued by drawing. The application period for deer is early September; bear license applications are due in early May. Preference points are awarded to unsuccessful applicants for both deer and bear. Hunters may choose either quota or no-quota areas for bear hunting. Minnesota usually holds a moose hunt every other year in early October. A limited number of elk licenses are also issued either yearly or every other year, depending on population fluctuations. Elk licenses are one per lifetime. Elk and Moose licenses are available only to residents and are distributed via drawing. Generally, hunters may only take one deer per year. Intensive harvest permits (anterless-only) are available for some areas. Regulations and season information are available on-line. Minnesota has over 11 million acres open to public hunting. Consisting of state and national forests and wildlife refuges, map information is available on-line. Information on hunter success, density, days hunted, and harvest information is also available on-line.

## Seasons

**Archery** - Minnnesota's archery deer season runs from the middle of September through the end of December for most of the state, with either sex harvest permitted in most zones.

**Muzzleloader** - Muzzleloader deer season is typically held in late November through mid-December. Sex restrictions vary by zones.

**Firearms** - Firearms deer seasons vary by zone and range from two to nine days and are held in November. Bear seasons are held from September through mid-October.

## Suggestions

Minnesota, with it's extensive public lands offers hunters the opportunity to hunt mature bucks in a wilderness setting. Deer numbers tend to be lower but good quality bucks are present.

For a true wilderness experience, try the Superior National Forest in the Northeast corner of the state - near Ely. You'll be hunting wilderness whitetails along with the wolves. Don't expect to see a lot of deer, but the quality of bucks you do see should be good. Don't overlook some of the larger State Forests either - George Washington State Forest and the Cloquet Valley State Forest are home to some trophy bucks as well!

# Missouri

Missouri Department of Conservation
P.O. Box 180
Jefferson City, MO 65102

Telephone: 573-751-4115
Web Page: http://www.conservation.state.mo.us/
E-mail: Internet@mail.conservation.state.mo.us

| Resident | Non-Resident |
| --- | --- |
| Whitetail Deer | Whitetail Deer |

The state is divided into 59 units for managing deer populations. Special regulations/seasons apply for individual units. Buck licenses for all units and any deer licenses for many units are available over the counter. Some units have limited quotas of any deer licenses that are issued via drawing - the application period is July 1 to August 15. Bonus antlerless deer licenses are available for some units. Missouri also offers numerous managed hunts which allow access to special areas not otherwise accessible. License numbers and harvest information can be accessed via the Internet. Licenses may be purchased over the phone using a credit card. Missouri's web page also contains information on public hunting areas and provides contact information for each unit. The database is searchable and contains maps for accessing each area.

## Seasons

**Archery** - Archery season typically starts October 1st and extends until January 15th. Archery season is closed during the firearms season.

**Muzzleloader** - Missouri has a 9-day muzzleloader season in December.

**Rifle** - Firearms season for deer consists of an 11-day season ending the Tuesday before Thanksgiving. Some units have an antlerless-only extension during January. This season typically covers the peak rut in Missouri.

## Suggestions

Missouri has a growing whitetail population and offers the opportunity to harvest multiple deer in many units. Archery recommendations include a hunt just before the firearms season - great pre-rut activity and late season archery hunts - hunters can harvest two deer - two bucks after the firearms season, and two turkeys. Firearm hunts in the northern portion of the state provide great opportunities for large bucks and hunters can typically take an additional antlerless deer (or two) with a bonus license. The managed hunts allow access to special areas and deer harvested on these hunts do not count towards the overall bag limits. Depending on unit hunted and licenses bought/drawn, hunters can harvest from 3 to 13 deer per year!

# Nebraska

Nebraska Game & Fish Commission
2200 N. 33rd Street
Lincoln, Nebraska 68503

Telephone: 402-471-0641
Web Page: www.ngpc.state.ne.us/
E-mail: Available through web page

| Resident | Non-Resident |
|---|---|
| Antelope | Antelope |
| Bighorn Sheep | - |
| Elk | - |
| Mule Deer | Mule Deer |
| Whitetail Deer | Whitetail Deer |

Archery and muzzleloader deer licenses are available to residents and non-residents for most units. Firearms deer licenses are available via drawing and over-the-counter to residents first (in April and May) and then via mail or over-the-counter to both residents and nonresidents in July. Archery antelope licenses are available to residents and non-residents. Rifle antelope licenses are issued via drawing to residents first, with the remaining licenses available to residents and nonresidents on a first come/first serve basis. Preference points are utilized for distributing antelope licenses. A very limited number of elk licenses are available to residents only via a drawing, with applications due in April/May. Bighorn sheep licenses (two in 1999) are available via lottery and auction. Nebraska requires hunter educations for all hunters born after January 1, 1977.

## Seasons

**Archery** - Archery seasons start in late August for antelope, September for deer and extending through December. Varies by species and area. Archery season typically closes during firearm seasons.

**Muzzleloader** - Antelope season is typically held in mid to late September. Deer season is usually the first two weeks of December.

**Rifle** - Regular and late firearm seasons are held for deer and antelope. Deer seasons occur in mid-November, with the late season in January. Antelope season is held during mid-October, with the late season beginning in early December and extending through January. Elk seasons typically starts in September/October and extend into November with another hunting period in late November/early December through late December. Bighorn sheep are hunted during a three-week season in December.

## Suggestions

Nebraska offers an excellent opportunity for a combination hunt - deer and upland game/waterfowl. Much of the best deer cover is located along rivers and streams which also offer good waterfowl and pheasant hunting. Their website includes a database of properties open to public hunting and includes property size, habitat types, and species available. It provides a good starting point for locating areas to hunt. Private property offers excellent trophy potential.

# North Dakota

North Dakota Game and Fish Department
100 N. Bismarck Expressway
Bismarck, ND 58501-5095

Telephone: (701) 328-6300
Web Page: http://www.state.nd.us/gnf/
E-mail: ndgf@state.nd.us

| Resident | Non-Resident |
|---|---|
| Antelope | - |
| Bighorn Sheep | Bighorn Sheep |
| Elk | - |
| Moose | - |
| Mule Deer | Mule Deer |
| Whitetail Deer | Whitetail Deer |

North Dakota offers opportunities primarily for deer - whitetails statewide and mule deer in the West and Southwest.

Unlimited archery licenses for whitetail deer are available with a limited number of "Any Deer" permits (valid for Mule or Whitetail deer) are available. Firearms licenses are limited for both residents and non-residents - in 1999, 86,000+ licenses were issued. Muzzleloader licenses are limited to 2% of the firearm licenses. Resident antelope hunters may hunt archery or firearms season. Non residents can only hunt antelope with archery equipment. Residents have limited opportunities for elk, moose and bighorn sheep - all of which are "once in a lifetime" licenses. Application dates vary by species and unit - usually March through June. Non-residents can participate in a lottery for one Bighorn Sheep license. Hunter education is required of those born after 1961.

North Dakota offers instant licensing available by calling 1-800-406-6409. Any time day or night, licenses can be purchased with a credit card. Instant Licensing is not available for licenses requiring a tag, such as for antelope and deer archery, because you must have the tag in your possession when in the field. You can still buy these licenses through Instant Licensing but must wait for them to arrive in the mail before they may be used.

## Seasons

**Archery** - Antelope archery season is typically split with a late August to mid-September season and a second season in October. Deer season typically starts in early September and extends through December.

**Muzzleloader** - North Dakota's special muzzleloader season is only open for deer hunting in late November to early December.

**Rifle** - Firearms season for antelope is early October. Deer season is generally early to mid-November.

## Suggestions

North Dakota also offers good small game hunting - pheasants, grouse, and waterfowl. A great strategy for non-residents is to combine big game hunting and bird hunting. A number of outfitters and landowners can provide services. Public land consisting of National Wildlife Refuges, Waterfowl Production Areas, State School Lands, and National Grasslands offer combination hunt possibilities.

Ohio Division of Wildlife
1840 Belcher Drive
Columbus, OH 43224

Telephone: 614-265-6565
Web Page: www.dnr.state.oh.us/odnr/wildlife
E-mail: Not Available

| Resident | Non-Resident |
|---|---|
| Whitetail Deer | Whitetail Deer |

Deer licenses are available over the counter or may be bought through the mail. Whitetail deer are found statewide. Hunters may harvest up to six deer, only one of which may be antlered. Deer bag limits and seasons are controlled by county. Urban deer permits are available for antlerless deer. Baiting is legal in Ohio. Hunters buying their first license are required to have a Hunter Safety Card. Regulations are available on-line. Ohio has numerous state wildlife areas, state forests, and state parks for hunters without access to private property. Their web page allows hunters to access this information and includes tract size, maps, contact information, etc.

## Seasons

**Archery** - Ohio has a long archery season - starting in early October and continuing through January. Crossbows may be used during the archery season.

**Muzzleloader** - There are two primitive weapons seasons - an early season for special areas held in late October and the statewide season held in late December/early January.

**Firearms** - Firearms deer season is typically held in late November and early December and typically runs for 6 to 7 days, depending on zone. Only shotguns and handguns may be used to hunt deer in Ohio.

## Suggestions

Ohio has good trophy potential, especially in agricultural areas. Many of the public areas are old strip mined areas or other areas with prime habitat. I suggest researching the maps available on the website and targeting some of the larger tracts. Be willing to go beyond where other hunters are willing to walk and your chances improve dramatically. With the short firearm season and the fact that crossbows are legal during archery seasons, a crossbow deer hunt is a unique opportunity. Private landowners are also typically more receptive to hunters using primitive weapons.

Oklahoma Department of Wildlife Conservation
1801 North Lincoln
Oklahoma City, OK 73105

Telephone: 405-521-3852
Web Page: www.wildlifedepartment.com
E-mail: pmoore@odwc.state.ok.us

| Resident | Non-Resident |
|---|---|
| Antelope | - |
| Elk | Elk |
| Whitetail Deer | Whitetail Deer |

Oklahoma has had record deer harvests 13 out of the last 15 years. They have also dramatically improved the age structure, with nearly 50% of the adult bucks 2½ years old or older. Deer licenses may be purchased over the counter. The annual bag limit is 5 deer, three of which may be bucks. Deer seasons are set statewide, with the antlerless harvest controlled by antlerless hunting days which vary from one day to the entire primitive and modern firearms seasons. Elk are found on private land in three counties in central Oklahoma. Licenses are issued to hunters with landowner permission in these areas. Oklahoma has 66 Wildlife Management Areas providing opportunity across the state. Most areas are located in the eastern portion of the state. Deer hunting is controlled on some areas and restrictions on antlerless deer hunting vary by area.

Oklahoma has 1.6 million acres of public land available with maps and contact information available through their web-page and via an atlas. Oklahoma offers a number of con-trolled hunts with licenses issues through a computerized drawing. They have a preference point system which increases your odds of drawing a license. Applications are due in May with results in June/July. Elk and Antelope licenses can only be drawn every ten years. There are typ-ically 200 elk licenses and 100 antelope licenses available each year.

## Seasons

**Archery** - Archery deer season starts in early October and runs through late December. It is closed during the firearms season. Hunters may take four deer per year (up to three bucks), subject to annual bag limits. Short archery elk seasons are held in early October and mid-December.

**Muzzleloader** - Oklahoma's muzzleloader deer season is held in late October through early November. One buck and one antlerless deer (on designated days and areas) may be taken per season.

**Firearms** - Firearms deer season occurs from mid to late November. One buck and one antlerless deer (on designated days and areas) may be taken per season. Short firearms elk seasons are held in early October and mid-December.

## Suggestions

Oklahoma's muzzleloader season occurs during the pre-rut - a time of high buck activity. Typically hunter numbers are less than during traditional firearms seasons, reducing hunter competition and pressure. Also, many of the controlled hunts offer good trophy potential and typically have high success rates. Two Wildlife Management Areas offer more than 700,000 acres of excellent deer hunting. The Honobia Creek and Three Rivers WMAs are located in the southeast part of the state and provide a wide variety of hunting opportunities. A special lands access permit is required for all hunters on this area. Look at the more remote area for less hunting pressure and more mature bucks.

South Dakota Department of Game Fish and Parks
523 East Capitol Avenue
Pierre, SD 57501-3182

Telephone: 605-773-3381
Web Page: http://www.state.sd.us/gfp/
E-mail: Wildinfo@gfp.state.sd.us

| Resident | Non-Resident |
|---|---|
| Antelope | - |
| Bighorn Sheep | - |
| Elk | - |
| Mountain Goat | - |
| Mule Deer | Mule Deer |
| Whitetail Deer | Whitetail Deer |

The state is divided into three regions for big game management - East River, West River, and the Black Hills.

Special regulations/seasons apply for certain counties and individual units. All big-game licenses are distributed via drawing. Drawing odds and drawing success can be accessed via the Internet. Application dates vary by species and unit - usually May through July. Bighorn sheep and mountain goat are "once in a lifetime" licenses. Some elk licenses are also once in a lifetime, with the remainder once per nine years.

## Seasons

**Archery** - Archery antelope season starts in mid-August and runs through late October. Deer seasons start in late September or early October and extend through late December. Elk archery seasons are held in September or November/December depending on unit.

**Muzzleloader** - South Dakota's special muzzleloader deer season is only open to residents and occurs in mid to late December.

**Rifle** - Firearms season for antelope are held in early October. Deer seasons in November and early December represent the majority of rifle hunting opportunities. Season length varies from 5 to 30+ days, depending on unit. Elk seasons are held in September, October, November, December, and January, depending on unit. Bighorn sheep and mountain goat seasons occur in mid to late October, with a January bighorn sheep hunt being held in Custer State Park.

## Suggestions

South Dakota is world renown for upland game hunting - pheasants, grouse, and waterfowl. A great strategy for non-residents is to combine big game hunting and bird hunting. A number of outfitters and landowners can provide services. Nearly 4.5 million acres of public land consisting of National Wildlife Refuges, the Black Hills, Waterfowl Production Areas, Walk-in Areas, and Game Production Areas offer combination hunt possibilities. A brochure describing the opportunities, locations and size of these areas in available by mail or on-line.

Texas Parks and Wildlife Department
4200 Smith School Road
Austin, Texas 78744

Telephone: 800-792-1112
Web Page: www.tpwd.state.tx.us/
E-mail: Available via web page

| Resident | Non-Resident |
| --- | --- |
| Antelope | Antelope |
| Desert Bighorn | Desert Bighorn |
| Mule Deer | Mule Deer |
| Whitetail Deer | Whitetail Deer |

Texas boasts the nation's largest Whitetail deer herd, with deer found in nearly every county statewide. Mule deer are found primarily in the southern and western portions of the state. Seasons and bag limits are controlled by county, with bag limits ranging from one to five deer in most counties.

All antelope and desert bighorn licenses are distributed to private landowners - hunter must make arrangements through these landowners. Regulations are available on-line.

Texas has more than 750,000 acres of public land available in 50 Wildlife Management Areas. Special regulations apply at many of these areas and drawings are used to control hunting pressure and harvest on many areas. Wildlife Management Area information including size and directions are available on-line.

## Seasons

All seasons are set by county. The following generalizations will provide an overview of the season structures.

**Archery** - Archery deer season is typically held in October.

**Muzzleloader** - Pure muzzleloader hunting opportunities are limited although muzzleloaders may be used throughout the long firearms season.

**Firearms** - Firearms deer season typically starts in mid November and extends into mid-January. Some counties have a late antlerless-only season starting in mid-January and running through late-January. Antelope season is held in early October.

## Suggestions

Much of the private property in Texas is intensively managed for whitetail deer. Part of this effort includes the taking of management bucks to improve the gene pool. Hunts for management bucks represent one of the best values in hunting today, with hunters often having the opportunity to take a good buck and experience Texas deer hunting. Antelope hunting on private land in the western and Panhandle regions also offers a chance at trophy bucks without a lot of hunting pressure. Expect to pay for almost any private land hunting opportunity and be sure that you understand what you are getting.

# Wisconsin

Wisconsin Department of Natural Resources
P.O. Box 7924
Madison, WI 53707

Telephone: 608-266-2621
Web Page: www.dnr.state.wi.us/
E-mail: wildlife@mail01.dnr.state.wi.us

| Resident | Non-Resident |
|---|---|
| Bear | Bear |
| Whitetail Deer | Whitetail Deer |

Wisconsin is divided into more than 80 units for deer management and three zones for bear management. Seasons and limits are controlled by zone. Antlerless deer harvest is also controlled by unit and through the issuance of Hunters Choice permits and bonus permits. Hunters Choice permits allow hunters to take a buck or doe, while bonus permits are antlerless only. These permits are issues by drawing with applications due in late July. Deer hunters may be restricted to shotguns in some counties during the firearms season. All bear licenses are issued via drawing, with applications due in mid-January. Preference points are used to distribute bear licenses. Hunters may use dogs and bait for bear hunting in some zones during specific portions of the season. Over the counter licenses may be purchased by phone or by mail. Harvest information and population maps are available on-line. Hunter education is required for persons born on or after January 1, 1973.

Wisconsin has over 200 state forests and wildlife areas offering nearly 500,000 acres available for hunting, with some information available through the web page. They also offer numerous special hunts on military bases, National Wildlife Refuges, State Parks, and other areas. National Forests also offer good hunting opportunities.

## Seasons

**Archery** - Wisconsin's archery deer season is split, with an early segment starting in mid-September and running through mid-November and the late season starting in early December and continuing through late December.

**Muzzleloader** - Muzzleloader deer season is held in late November through early December.

**Firearms** - Firearms deer season starts in mid-November and runs through late November. Some units have late antlerless only seasons. Season length is set by zone. Bear season starts in early September and runs through mid-October. Baiting and dog hunting season are typically shorter.

## Suggestions

Wisconsin has a growing bear population and is trying to increase the harvest, especially in the northwestern portion of the state. An early September bear hunt over bait is a good prospect. The Cheqaumegon National Forest provides good access to this area. Deer hunting is good throughout the state, with the special hunts offering good opportunities and high success potential. Waterfowl hunting and an archery deer hunt is a good way to sample the best Wisconsin has to offer. The Northern Highland State Forest is a good place to try a combination deer/duck hunt.

# Southeast

Alabama, Arkansas, Florida, Georgia, Louisana, Mississippi, North Carolina, South Carolina, Tennesse

The southeastern United States is a deer hunter's mecca. With long seasons and liberal bag limits - a buck a day in Alabama, hunters can use a variety of methods - stand hunting, drives, and dogs to take America's favorite game animal - the whitetail deer. Bear hunting is good in the northern part of this region. A variety of terrain awaits hunters in this region. The mountains of western North Carolina and eastern Tennessee offer ridges over 5000 feet above sea level, while all the coastal states have thick swamps and marshes near sea level. Things happen a little later in this part of the country - the rut typically occurs in December and January in the southern part of this region, so plan accordingly. Many states also have very good duck hunting - making a great combination hunt possible.

Alabama Division of Wildlife & Freshwater Fisheries
64 North Union Street
Montgomery, AL 36130

Telephone: 334-242-3465
Web Page: www.dcnr.state.al.us/agfd
E-mail: Available through web page

| Resident | Non-Resident |
|---|---|
| Whitetail Deer | Whitetail Deer |

Deer seasons are set by county in Alabama. The limit is one buck per day. Hunters Choice days allow hunters to harvest an antlerless deer in addition to the one buck per day. The number of Hunter Choice days varies from three to 45, depending on county. Most public lands are restricted to three Hunters Choice days per year. Hunters may use dogs to hunt deer in select counties.

Alabama has more than 600,000 acres of public property in 33 Wildlife Management Areas. Most are open to deer hunting. Wildlife Management Area information including species present, size, special regulations, directions and contact information is available on-line. Alabama also has several National Forests open to hunting. Licenses may be purchased by phone or over the counter. Hunter education is required for persons born on or after August 1, 1977.

## Seasons

**Archery** - Alabama's archery deer season starts in mid- to late October and typically runs through the end of January. Hunters may take one deer per day of either sex.

**Muzzleloader** - Alabama only offers a special muzzle-loader season on private property and select public lands from mid to late January. Hunters may take two deer per day - one buck and one doe.

**Firearms** - Firearms season typically opens in late November and runs through the end of January. Hunting with dogs (where permitted) occurs during the first part of the season.

## Suggestions

With deer densities greater than 30 deer per square mile, southern Alabama is an ideal location to take advantage of the liberal bag limits. Hunters wanting to harvest antlerless deer can usually find access to private property. Hunting on most Wildlife Management Areas is also good for bucks. The W.L. Holland & Mobile-Tensaw Delta Wildlife Management Area, with over 58,000 acres and lots of marsh and wetlands, is a great location for a combination deer and duck hunt. Deer hunting is restricted to the end of the week and weekends. Arrive early, hunt ducks in the morning and evening, scouting for deer at mid-day. Switch to deer hunting when it opens on the weekend.

# Arkansas

Arkansas Game & Fish Commission
#2 Natural Resources Drive
Little Rock AR 72205

Telephone: 501-223-6300
Web Page: www.agfc.com
E-mail: Not Available

| Resident | Non-Resident |
| --- | --- |
| Bear | Bear |
| Elk | - |
| Whitetail Deer | Whitetail Deer |

Deer and bear licenses are available over the counter or may be bought over the phone. Elk licenses are totally limited. Whitetail deer are found statewide. Hunters may harvest up to four deer per year - not more than two bucks. A three antler-point restriction on bucks helps encourage hunters to harvest more mature deer. Dogs may be used to hunt deer in some units. Bears may not be hunted over bait or with dogs. Hunters born after December 31, 1968 are required to have a Hunter Safety card. Regulations and harvest results are available on-line. Arkansas has more than 100 public hunting areas available, with maps, species, size, directions, and nearby facility information available on-line. Special regulations may apply at Wildlife Management Areas. Arkansas offers both three and five-day licenses which allow hunters to take both deer and bear, in addition to small game.

## Seasons

**Archery** - Arkansas' archery seasons vary by units. Seasons start in early October and run through early January or February, depending on units. Crossbows may be used during the entire archery season.

**Muzzleloader** - Two muzzleloader seasons are held for deer. The first is in early October and a late season is held in late December/early January.

**Firearms** - Firearms deer season typically starts in mid-November and extends into early December. There is also a Christmas deer hunt - starting right after Christmas and running for three days. Bear seasons are held in October and November, with dates varying by method and zone. Elk season consists of two 5 day hunts - one in September and a second in December.

## Suggestions

With short duration licenses available over the counter and long deer seasons, Arkansas is a good choice for a quick trip. If you have a crossbow, Arkansas in late October or early November is prime time to harvest a pre-rut whitetail with a unique historic weapon. Arkansas has decent trophy potential, with the antler-point restrictions improving the age structure. The Christmas deer season offers hunters an opportunity to take the kids hunting during Christmas break. Another possibility is to hunt the later portion of the archery season. With seasons extending into January and February, it is a great cure for cabin fever!

# Florida

Florida Fish & Wildlife Conservation Commission
620 South Meridian Street
Tallahassee, FL 32399

Telephone: Numerous Regional Offices
Web Page: www.state.fl.us/fwc
E-mail: Available through web page

| Resident | Non-Resident |
|---|---|
| Whitetail Deer | Whitetail Deer |

Deer seasons are set by zone in Florida. The limit is two bucks per day with an annual limit of 4. Two antlerless deer may be taken by bow and one with firearms during the antlerless season. Hunters may use dogs to hunt deer in most areas.

Florida has more than 125 Wildlife Management Areas - some exceeding 500,000 acres. Most are open to deer hunting. Wildlife Management Area information including maps, species present, size, special regulations, directions and contact information is available on-line. Florida also has several National Forests open to hunting. Licenses may be purchased over the counter. Hunter education is required for persons born on or after June 1, 1975.

## Seasons

**Archery** - Florida's archery deer seasons start from early September through mid-October and close from early October through mid-November. Hunters may take deer of either sex.

**Muzzleloader** - Muzzleloader seasons are three to nine-day seasons held in October and mid-November.

**Firearms** - Firearms season typically opens in late October or mid-November and runs into early to late January. Hunting with dogs is permitted in most areas.

## Suggestions

Florida allows archery and muzzleloader hunters the opportunity to take turkeys (gobblers only) during the archery and muzzleloader deer seasons. This unique opportunity makes these seasons very attractive. The large tracts of public land provide ample opportunity to get away from the crowds. Combined with warm weather, hunters can hunt both species and enjoy fishing, golf or any of the other attractions Florida offers.

Georgia Department of Natural Resources - Wildlife Resources
142 Bob Kirk Rd NW
Thomson, GA 30824

Telephone: 706-667-4672
Web Page: www.dnr.state.ga.us/dnr/wild/
E-mail: Not Available

| Resident | Non-Resident |
|---|---|
| Bear | Bear |
| Whitetail Deer | Whitetail Deer |

Deer and bear licenses are available over the counter or may be bought over the phone, by mail, or through the Internet. Whitetail deer and bear are found statewide. Hunters may harvest up to eight deer per year - only two may be antlered. Some counties have antler point or spread restrictions designed to shift the harvest towards mature bucks. Dogs may be used to hunt bear in the southern zone. Regulations and season information are available on-line. Georgia has 90 public hunting areas available, with maps, size, directions, and special regulations available on-line. Hunter education is required for hunters born on or after January 1, 1961.

## Seasons

**Archery** - Georgia's archery deer season varies by county. Seasons typically start in mid-September and extend through the end of December in some counties. Other counties close in mid-October and reopen for a week in late October. Deer of either sex may be taken during archery hunts. A separate archery season for bear is held only in the Northern Zone. It starts in mid-September and extends into mid October.

**Muzzleloader** - Muzzleloader deer season is typically seven days in length and is held in mid-October. During the first two days, deer of either sex may be taken. Only bucks may be taken during the remainder of the season.

**Firearms** - Firearms deer season typically starts in late October and extends to early January. Season length varies by zone and the antlerless deer harvest is controlled by county. Antlerless deer may be harvested on either-sex days as designated by county, with the number of days varying from 0 to the entire season - 53 days in the southern zone during 1999. Firearms bear seasons vary by zone. The Northern Zone season typically starts in early November and runs through early December. In the Southern Zone, three two-day seasons are held in late-September and early October. Dogs may be used in the Southern Zone.

## Suggestions

Georgia's long firearms season offer hunters an opportunity to hunt a variety of conditions. The pre-rut and rut periods are probably the most popular, but hunters should not overlook the early portion of the season, when deer can be patterned around food sources. Many of the Wildlife Management Areas have food plots or agricultural crops, providing good opportunities to hunters without access to private property. Another interesting possibility is a combination bear and deer hunt in either the Northern or Southern Zone.

# Louisiana

Louisiana Department of Wildlife & Fisheries
P.O. Box 98000
Baton Rouge, LA 70898

Telephone: 225-765-2360
Web Page: www.wlf.state.la.us
E-mail: Various - available from web page

| Resident | Non-Resident |
| --- | --- |
| Whitetail Deer | Whitetail Deer |

Deer licenses are available over the counter or may be bought through the mail or over the phone. Whitetail deer are found statewide. Hunters may harvest up to six deer per year and up to two per day (when legal). Either sex days, 5 to 13 per unit, are used to control the antlerless harvest. Dogs may be used to hunt deer in certain units during specified times. Hunters born on or after September 1, 1969 are required to have a Hunter Safety card. Regulations are available on-line. Louisiana has 47 Wildlife

Management Areas for hunters without access to private property. Their web page allows hunters to access this information and includes maps, tract size, and contact information. Special regulations apply on some areas.

## Seasons

**Archery** - Archery seasons vary by unit - starting in either mid September or early October and extending until either mid or late January.

**Muzzleloader** - The muzzleloader seasons for deer are either-sex statewide and vary by unit. Typically there is an early season in October/November and a late season in December/January.

**Firearms** - Firearms deer seasons also vary by unit, with split seasons occurring from October through January. Either-sex days are scattered throughout these split seasons.

## Suggestions

Louisiana offers an excellent opportunity for a combination hunts - deer and ducks. Many of the public areas are large properties and are perfect for combination hunts. Be aware that some areas are very swampy and may be difficult to access. Many of the Wildlife Management Areas limit deer harvest to bucks only. With the late seasons, and the timing of the rut in Louisiana (January), hunters can plan a trip and hunt rutting deer long after northern seasons are closed. With burgeoning duck and snow goose populations, combination hunts are a perfect cure for cabin fever.

Mississippi Department of Wildlife, Fish & Parks
P.O. Box 451
Jackson, MS 39205

Telephone: 601-362-9212
Web Page: www.mdwfp.com
E-mail: Available through web page

| Resident | Non-Resident |
| --- | --- |
| Whitetail Deer | Whitetail Deer |

Deer licenses are available over the counter or may be bought through the mail or over the phone. Whitetail deer are found statewide. Resident hunters may harvest one buck per day and one antlerless deer per day when permitted - up to three bucks and five antlerless deer per year. Two additional antlerless deer may be taken during archery seasons. Either-sex days for specific areas are used to control the antlerless deer harvest. Nonresident hunters may take a buck per day - three per year and may only harvest antlerless deer on property they own or lease. Dogs may be used to hunt deer in certain units during specified times. Hunters born after January 1, 1972 are required to have a Hunter Safety card. Regulations are available on-line. Mississippi has 42 Wildlife Management Areas covering more than 800,000 acres for hunters without access to private property. Their web page allows hunters to access this information and includes maps, tract size, and contact information. Special regulations apply on some areas. Harvest information is also available on-line.

## Seasons

**Archery** - Archery season is typically held from early October through mid-November.

**Muzzleloader** - The muzzleloader season for deer is held from early to mid-December. Deer of either sex can be taken with primitive weapons.

**Firearms** - Firearms deer seasons also vary by hunting methods - hunters using dogs may hunt during late-November until early December and again from late December through mid-January. Dogs may not be used during the firearms season starting in mid-December and running approximately 8 days.

## Suggestions

Mississippi offers an excellent opportunity for a combination hunts - deer and ducks. Many of the public areas are large properties and are perfect for combination hunts. Be aware that some areas are very swampy and may be difficult to access. Mississippi also offers hunters the opportunity to hunt deer using dogs - a real delight to many. With long seasons, hunters can plan a trip to Mississippi around the Thanksgiving or Christmas holidays. A special youth hunt in mid-November is a great way to spend time with younger hunters and mentor them.

# North Carolina

North Carolina Wildlife Resources Commission
512 North Salisbury Street
Raleigh, NC 27604

Telephone: 919-733-3391
Web Page: www.wildlife.state.nc.us
E-mail: Not Available

| Resident | Non-Resident |
|---|---|
| Bear | Bear |
| Whitetail Deer | Whitetail Deer |

Deer and bear licenses are available over the counter or may be bought over the phone. Whitetail deer and bear are found statewide. Hunters may harvest up to two deer per day and six deer per year - at least two must be antlerless. Dogs may be used to hunt bear in some units. Regulations and season information are available on-line. Hunting is prohibited on Sundays. North Carolina has more than two million acres of game lands available throughout the state. A special license is required. General information for game lands is available - open days, deer seasons, etc. Numerous bear sanctuaries are closed to bear hunting. Dogs may be used to hunt bears in most areas. Baiting is not permitted. Deer may be hunted with dogs in most areas during the firearm season only.

## Seasons

**Archery** - North Carolina's archery deer season consists of an early segment from mid-September through early October and a late segment starting in late October and running through late November. Either sex of deer may be taken.

**Muzzleloader** - Muzzleloader deer season is typically either mid October or mid November. Sex restrictions vary by county.

**Firearms** - Firearms deer season typically starts in late November and extends into mid-December. Seasons are set by region with either sex seasons set by county and vary from bucks only to either sex harvest permitted for the entire season. Bear seasons are held in November and December, with dates varying by zone.

## Suggestions

In the east, try the Croatan National Forest for deer. Some of the eastern swamps offer good bear hunting with hounds. The Pisgah National Forest west of Lenoir offers good deer and bear hunting, with combination hunts a good prospect. With mountains above 6000 feet, hunters can find as rugged of country as they wish. The extreme south-western corner of the state offers good hunting in the Nantahala National Forest. Focusing on food sources - mast and agricultural crops for both deer and bears is a good strategy in all seasons.

# South Carolina

South Carolina Department of Natural Resources
Rembert C. Dennis Building
1000 Assembly Street
Columbia, SC 29201

Telephone: 803-734-3888
Web Page: www.dnr.state.sc.us/
E-mail: Available through web page

| Resident | Non-Resident |
| --- | --- |
| Bear | Bear |
| Whitetail Deer | Whitetail Deer |

South Carolina has some of the longest deer seasons and most liberal bag limits in the nation. The State is divided into 11 Game Zones for management purposes. Deer licenses are available over the counter. Whitetail deer are found statewide. Hunters may harvest five bucks in most Game Zones, with some zones having no limits on bucks.

Most Wildlife Management Areas have more restrictive limits on both bucks and antlerless deer. Either-sex hunts are established by county and may be further limited on Wildlife Management Areas. Dogs may be used to hunt deer in certain units during specified times. Hunters born after June 30, 1979 are required to have a Hunter Safety card. Regulations and season information are available on-line. South Carolina has more than 1.2 million acres for hunters without access to private property. These range in size from several hundred acres to more than 350,000 acres. Their web page allows hunters to access this information and includes maps, species present, tract size, and contact information. Special regulations apply on most areas. Harvest information is also available on-line.

## Seasons

**Archery** - Archery seasons vary widely by Game Zone and Wildlife Management Areas. Seasons start as early as mid-August with closing dates ranging from October through January.

**Muzzleloader** -Muzzleloader seasons for deer start in mid-September and close from October through mid-November. Some Wildlife Management Areas have late seasons in December.

**Firearms** - Firearms deer seasons also vary widely by unit and hunting method. Some seasons start as early as mid August, with most units open during all or parts of October, November, and December. Hunters using dogs are typically restricted to shorter periods throughout the season. Bear hunting is available only in Game Zone 1, with a still hunt season preceding the dog hunt season. Both hunts are held in October and are typically 6 days long.

## Suggestions

South Carolina offers long seasons and liberal bag limits for deer. For hunters using dogs, a combination deer and hog hunt is a unique opportunity. Many of the public areas are large properties and are perfect for combination hunts. An early archery hunt offers the opportunity to take deer with antlers still in velvet. Hunting some of the larger Wildlife Management Areas offers the opportunity for hunters to get away from pressure.

# Tennessee

Tennessee Wildlife Resource Agency
P.O. Box 40747
Nashville, TN 37204

Telephone: 615-781-6500
Web Page: www.state.tn.us/twra
E-mail: Available through web page

| Resident | Non-Resident |
|---|---|
| Bear | Bear |
| Whitetail Deer | Whitetail Deer |

Tennessee is divided into two units for deer management, with bag limits varying from one to four per year, depending on zone and weapon type. Hunters may only take three antlered bucks per year, not more than two per weapon type, and only one per day. Deer taken during special antlerless-only hunts typically do not count towards the annual bag limit. Antlerless deer harvest is controlled by season and county, with quota permits required for many counties and seasons. Up to three antlerless deer may be harvested, depending on county. Bear seasons and methods are established by county, with dogs permitted in most open counties. Hunter education is required for persons born on or after January 1, 1969.

Tennessee has 87 Wildlife Management Areas and refuges across the state ranging in size from 88 to 625,000 acres. All of these properties are open to public hunting, although regulations apply at many Wildlife Management Areas and special permits may be required, depending on season and hunting methods. A number of cooperative properties (usually owned by timber companies) are open to hunting, subject to special permits and regulations.

## Seasons

**Archery** - Tennessee's archery deer season starts in late September and extends to early November in both units. Later archery hunts are typically held in November and December around the muzzleloader and firearms seasons in the western part of the state. An archery-only bear season is held in two counties in eastern Tennessee in mid to late October.

**Muzzleloader** - Two muzzleloader deer seasons are held - one before firearms season and one after. The early season is held from early to mid-November and usually runs for seven days. The late season is held from early through mid-December, with durations ranging between three and seven days.

**Firearms** - There are usually two split firearms deer seasons - one held from late November through early December and a second hunt held in late December to early January. Firearms bear seasons are held in either late September or early December with durations from five to 14 days, depending on county.

## Suggestions

Many of the larger Wildlife Management Areas do not have quotas on the number of deer hunters and provide the opportunity to get away from hunters. The first muzzle-loader season is a good time to hunt for pre-rut and rutting whitetails. Another possibility is a combination waterfowl and archery deer hunt at the 24,000 acre Reelfoot Wildlife Management Area located in Western Tennessee.

Connecticut, Delaware, Kentucky, Maine, Maryland, Massachusetts, New Hampshire, New Jersey, New York, Pennsylvania, Rhode Island, Vermont, Virginia, West Virginia

The northeastern United States typically isn't considered a "destination" location for big game hunters from other parts of the country. Hunters who summarily dismiss this region are overlooking some great hunting opportunities. Whitetail deer are found in every state in the region, with long seasons and liberal bag limits in many areas. Bear and moose populations are strong in many states, with great hunting opportunities available on public land. Since parts of this region are heavily populated, special methods are often required to improve the safety of hunting near population centers. Public land is plentiful in almost every state, with tract size ranging from tens of acres to millions. Smaller tracts may require hunters to change their approach to hunting, focusing more on stand hunting.

Connecticut Department of Environmental Protection
Wildlife Division
79 Elm Street
Hartford, CT 06106

Telephone: 860-424-3011
Web Page: www.dep.state.ct.us/burnatr/wildlife
E-mail: Not Available

| Resident | Non-Resident |
|---|---|
| Whitetail Deer | Whitetail Deer |

Deer licenses are available over the counter or through a lottery system for certain zones and public properties. Whitetail deer are found statewide. Deer bag limits and seasons vary based on hunting methods and public/private property. Legal hunting methods vary. Only shotguns or muzzleloaders may be used on State land. Rifles may be used on private property with the permission of the landowner. Some State lands are archery-only. All hunters are required to have a Hunter Safety Card or a previous Connecticut hunting license. Regulations are available on-line. Connecticut has numerous state wildlife areas, state forests, and state parks for hunters without access to private property. Access to many of these properties is controlled for deer hunting, with applications due in mid-March. Their web page allows hunters to access this information and includes tract size, species present, directions, and special permit restrictions.

## Seasons

**Archery** - Connecticut has split archery seasons with the first season typically starting in mid-September and running through mid-November. The second season starts either in mid-November or early December and runs through mid to late December.

**Muzzleloader** - Muzzleloader season typically runs 14 days from early to mid-December, with bags limits of one deer on State land or two on private property.

**Firearms** - Firearms deer season is typically held from mid-November until either late November or early December, depending on zone and property ownership.

## Suggestions

With lots of public land available for archery hunting and a four deer bag limit, archery hunters have lots of opportunities. I suggest public areas and planning a hunt for either late September or late October. The September hunt should offer a chance to enjoy the fall colors and hunt deer patterned on food sources. The late October hunt should hit the peak pre-rut and offer opportunities at deer all day long.

# Delaware

Delaware Division of Fish and WIldlife
89 Kings Highway
Dover, DE 19901

Telephone: 302-739-5297
Web Page: www.dnrec.state.de.us/fw/fwwel.htm
E-mail: Not Available

| Resident | Non-Resident |
|---|---|
| Whitetail Deer | Whitetail Deer |

Deer licenses are available over the counter or through a lottery system for Wildlife Management Areas. Whitetail deer are found statewide. Hunters may take two deer per year - total from all seasons. Only one buck may be taken in except for Quality Buck Tags. Seasons are set statewide. Legal hunting methods vary. Shotguns are the only legal modern firearm allowed in Delaware. Hunters born after January 1, 1967 are required to have a Hunter Safety Card. Regulations are available on-line. Licenses may be bought on-line and through the mail. Delaware has numerous Wildlife Management Areas providing nearly 50,000 acres of public hunting opportunity. Access to some of these areas is limited for deer hunting and hunters may be required to hunt from provided stands. Delaware's web page allows hunters to access Wildlife Management Area information including maps, size and special regulations. Harvest information is available on-line.

## Seasons

**Archery** - Delaware has a long archery season - starting in early September and running through the end of January. Hunters may take two deer, subject to annual bag limits.

**Muzzleloader** - Two muzzleloader seasons provide early and late season opportunities. The early season in held from early to mid-October. The late season is held in late January. Hunters may take two deer, subject to annual bag limits.

**Firearms** - Three firearm deer seasons are typically held. Two buck seasons are held - the first in mid-November and the second in mid-January. A special antlerless deer season is held in mid-December. Hunters may take two deer, subject to annual bag limits.

## Suggestions

With numerous public areas available and a long archery season, I suggest participating in drawings for public areas. sources. A late season muzzleloader hunt is a good cure for cabin fever.  The November buck season should hit the rut.  Look for bucks to move all day.  Find the does and the bucks will follow.

Kentucky Department of Fish & Wildlife Resources
#1 Game Farm Road
Frankfort, KY 40601

Telephone: 800-858-1549
Web Page: www.kdfwr.state.ky.us/
E-mail: Available through web page

| Resident | Non-Resident |
|---|---|
| Whitetail Deer | Whitetail Deer |

Kentucky is divided into six zones for deer management, with each county assigned a zone number. Seasons and limits are controlled by zone. Antlerless deer harvest is also controlled by zone. Hunters may take four deer per year, only one of which may be a buck. Kentucky also has 40 quota hunts throughout the state, offering a variety of opportunities to hunters. Hunter education is required for persons born on or after January 1, 1975.

Kentucky has 76 Wildlife Management Areas and State Forests throughout the state offering hunters numerous public land opportunities. Most of these properties are open to public hunting, although special regulations apply at many Wildlife Management Areas and special permits may be required, depending on season and hunting methods. On-line Wildlife Management Area information includes size, species present, ownership, and directions.

## Seasons

**Archery** - Kentucky's archery deer season starts in mid-September and continues through mid-January.

**Muzzleloader** - Two muzzleloader deer seasons are held - one before firearms season and one after. The early season is held in late October usually runs for two days. The late season is held in mid-December, and is usually seven days long.

**Firearms** - Firearms deer seasons start in mid-November and run through late November. Season length is set by zone.

## Suggestions

Kentucky's restrictive buck harvest policies have improved the trophy potential dramatically. About 10 Boone and Crockett bucks are taken every year. The Daniel Boone National Forest offers 670,000 acres of public hunting to hunters. Opportunities to get away from other hunters can be found by those willing to work harder. The early muzzleloader season offers a good chance at a pre-rut deer.

The long archery season offers the possibility for combination deer and waterfowl hunts - a great option in western Kentucky.

Maine Department of Inland Fisheries and Wildlife
284 State Street
41 StateHouse Station
Augusta, ME 04333

Telephone: 800-452-4664
Web Page: janus.state.me.us/ifw/index.htm
E-mail: Available through web

| Resident | Non-Resident |
|---|---|
| Bear | Bear |
| Moose | Moose |
| Whitetail Deer | Whitetail Deer |

Deer and bear licenses are available over the counter, with drawings held for special antlerless deer hunts. Moose licenses are distributed via lottery with a bonus point system improving your chances. Applications are due in early

April. Lottery results are available on-line. There is a two-year waiting period after drawing a moose license. The licensee and a single sub-permittee may hunt on each moose license. Seasons and antlerless deer permits are set based on Wildlife Management Districts. Hunters may take from one to three deer per year, depending on successfully drawing special licenses. Dogs and bait may be used to hunt bear, subject to specific restrictions and seasons.

Adult hunters are required to have a Hunter Safety Card or proof of holding an adult license. Regulations are available on-line. Licenses may be bought on-line. Maine has numerous Wildlife Management Areas and National Forests providing millions of acres of public hunting opportunity. Their web page allows hunters to access Wildlife Management Area information including descriptions, maps, size, habitat present and special regulations. Hunting is prohibited on Sundays.

## Seasons

**Archery** - Maine's archery deer season is typically held from late September through late October, with an expanded season in select Wildlife Management Districts from early September through early December.

**Muzzleloader** - Muzzleloader deer seasons are held from late November through early December. Some Wildlife Management Departments have a second season in early to mid-December.

**Firearms** - Firearm deer seasons are typically held in late October through late November. Bear season typically starts in late August and extends through late November, with baiting legal through late September. Dogs may be used from mid-September through late October. Moose season is held in early to mid-October.

## Suggestions

Try some of these Wildlife Management Areas for big Maine whitetails - Bud Leavitt Wildlife Management Area (6300 Acres), Alonzo H. Garcelon Wildlife Management Area (4300 acres), Steep Falls Wildlife Management Area (4900 acres), Lt. Gordon Manuel Wildlife Management Area (6400 acres), and the Mt Agamenticus Wildlife Management Area (1100 acres). The White Mountain National Forest near the border with New Hampshire is another good choice. If you want to track bucks in the snow, the muzzleloader season offers the best chance for tracking snow and there will be fewer hunters afield. The early archery season typically offers good weather and beautiful fall colors - try concentrating on food sources.

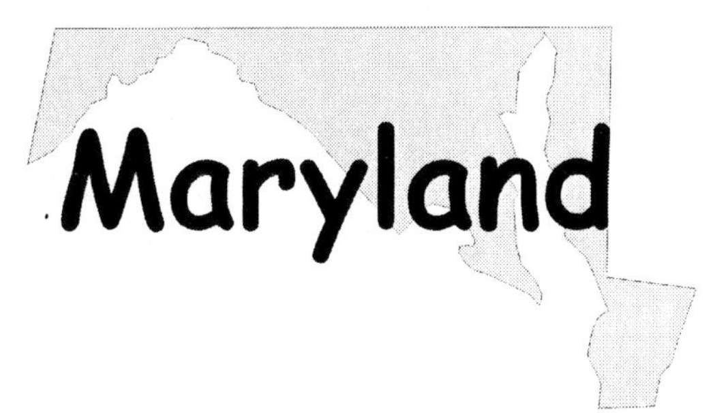


Maryland Wildlife and Heritage Division
580 Taylor Ave. E-1
Annapolis, MD 21401

Telephone: 410-260-8200
Web Page: www.dnr.state.md.us/wildlife/
E-mail: Available through Web Page

| Resident | Non-Resident |
|---|---|
| Whitetail Deer | Whitetail Deer |

Deer licenses are available over the counter and are valid for bucks in all Deer Management Regions and antlerless deer in most Regions. A lottery system is used for distributing some antlerless deer licenses. Whitetail deer are found statewide. Hunters may take from two to four deer per year by each method (bow, muzzleloader, and firearm) in each region - more than 30 deer per year! Seasons and bag limits are set by zone. There are some restrictions on the use of rifles in certain counties. Hunters born after July 1, 1977 are required to have a Hunter Safety Card or proof of a hunting license prior to 1977. Regulations are available on-line. Licenses may be bought through the mail. Maryland has numerous Wildlife Management Areas, State Parks and State Forests providing more than 100,000 acres of public hunting opportunity. Access to some of these areas is limited for deer hunting. Maryland's web page allows hunters to access Wildlife Management Area information including maps, size and special regulations. Hunting is prohibited on Sundays.

## Seasons

**Archery** - Maryland's archery season is typically divided into four segments - starting in mid-September and running through the end of January.

**Muzzleloader** - Two muzzleloader seasons provide early and late season opportunities. The early season is held in late October. The late season is held in mid to late December.

**Firearms** - Firearm deer seasons are typically held in late November through mid-December.

## Suggestions

Maryland is known for outstanding waterfowl hunting. The Frederick City Cooperative Wildlife Management Area offers over 7,000 acres with good deer hunting and numerous ponds for a pleasant combination hunt. Hunters wanting to get away from it all might try the Dan's Mountain

Wildlife Management Area located in the western part of the state. This Wildlife Management Area offers the largest contiguous state-owned forest in Maryland. At 9,200 acres, this area offers rugged hunting for deer.

# Massachusetts

Massachusetts Division of Fisheries & Wildlife
100 Cambridge Street, Room 1902
Boston, MA 02202

Telephone: 617-626-1591
Web Page: www.state.ma.us/dfwele/
E-mail: Available through web page

| Resident | Non-Resident |
| --- | --- |
| Bear | Bear |
| Whitetail Deer | Whitetail Deer |

Deer seasons are established by zone. Seasonal limits are two antlered deer or 1 antlered and one antlerless deer for all seasons combined - archery, muzzleloader, and shotgun. Additional antlerless deer may be taken in specific zones, depending on the deer population. Rifles may not be used for deer hunting. Deer permits may be purchased over the counter. Bear permits are available for specific counties through an application process prior to season opening and may be hunted with rifles, bow, pistol, and muzzleloaders. All hunting is prohibited on Sundays.

Massachusetts has more than 100 Wildlife Management Areas providing almost 100,000 acres of public hunting. Sixty-three more State Parks and Forests provide good hunting opportunities. Special restrictions may apply.

## Seasons

**Archery** - Massachusetts' archery deer season starts in either mid October or early November (depending on Zone) and closes in late November. Hunters may take deer of either sex, subject to the season bag limit.

**Muzzleloader** - The muzzleloader season is held in Mid-December. Hunters may take deer of either sex in most zones without a special permit, subject to the seasonal bag limit.

**Firearms** - Firearms season typically starts in late November and runs through early to mid-December, depending on Zone. Hunters are restricted to antlered deer only unless an antlerless deer permit is obtained via drawing.

## Suggestions

With the archery season coinciding with the pre-rut and rut, archery hunters have good opportunities on most of the public lands. By researching public areas and access, hunters can identify areas that meet their needs. Zones with a mid-October opening day offer good opportunities for hunting during the peak fall color season. Massachusetts closes all hunting seasons except waterfowl during the shotgun deer season.

# New Hampshire

New Hampshire Fish and Game Department
2 Hazen Drive
Concord, NH 03301

Telephone: 603-271-3211
Web Page: www.wildlife.state.nh.us/
E-mail: info@wildlife.state.nh.us

| Resident | Non-Resident |
| --- | --- |
| Bear | Bear |
| Moose | Moose |
| Whitetail Deer | Whitetail Deer |

All deer and bear licenses are available over the counter. Whitetail deer and bears are found statewide. Moose licenses are issued via drawing with applications typically due in late May. Two people may hunt moose on a single license - only one moose may be taken. Bears may be hunted with dogs and bait. Hunter education is required for all hunters.

## Seasons

**Archery** - Archery season for deer runs from mid-September through mid-December. Hunters may take deer of either sex.

**Muzzleloader** - The muzzleloader season for deer varies by Wildlife Management Unit and is held in late-October through early-November. Sex restrictions vary by unit.

**Firearms** - Firearms deer season typically starts in early November and runs through early December. Some units allow either sex harvest at the beginning of the firearms season. Hunters may only take one deer total during the firearms and muzzleloader seasons. Moose season is held in late October. Bear seasons vary by unit, starting in early September and closing in September, November or December. Baiting seasons are held early in the hunt and dogs may be used during some later segments.

## Suggestions

The White Mountain National Forest offers good deer and bear hunting and enough roads for good access. A bait or dog hunt for bears offers a good chance of success and is a great way to hunt bruins in the thick cover. The muzzle-loader deer season is timed to catch the pre-rut and rut. The firearms deer season is late enough to have several good tracking snows - some local hunters don't even start hunting until they get a good tracking snow.

# New Jersey


New Jersey Division of Fish and Wildlife
P.O. Box 400
Trenton, NJ 08625

Telephone: 609-292-2965
Web Page: www.state.nj.us/dep/fgw/hunting.htm
E-mail: Not Available


| Resident | Non-Resident |
|---|---|
| Whitetail Deer | Whitetail Deer |

Deer licenses are available over the counter or may be bought through the mail. Whitetail deer are found statewide. New Jersey has more than 60 deer zones used to control harvest and maintain population objectives. Special seasons are held for certain zones for both archery and firearms hunters. Bonus deer permits are often available for antlerless deer. Harvest information is available on-line. New Jersey has more that 750,000 acres of public land available for deer hunting. This includes 260,000 acres in 111 Wildlife Management Areas. Their web page allows hunters to access Wildlife Management Area information and includes tract size and county.

## Seasons

**Archery** - New Jersey has several archery seasons. The first season varies by zones and typically runs from mid-September through late October or early October through late October. A special permit archery season is held in some zones starting in late October and closing in either late November or late December. A statewide late archery season runs most of January.

**Muzzleloader** - A muzzleloader season for deer is held in most zones and usually includes two days in late-November and 12 days in December/January.

**Firearms** - A six-day state-wide firearms deer season is typically held in early to mid-December. Permit shotgun seasons are held in many zones. These seasons range in duration from 1 to 31 days and are held in late-November through late January.

## Suggestions

New Jersey has a strong deer population and lots of hunting opportunities on public land. In some zones, hunters can hunt more than 100 days and bag multiple deer. New Jersey's firearms seasons are typically held after the rut, making the regular archery season a good choice. Hunting food sources during the early part of the season should be very effective, with action picking up as the pre-rut turns on in late October. The permit archery season is a good opportunity to hunt rutting whitetails. In some locations, hunters are required to harvest an antlerless deer before taking a buck. Be sure that you understand the regulations for the season and area you select to hunt.

New York Department of Environmental Conservation
Bureau of Wildlife
50 Wolf Road
Albany, NY 12233

Telephone: 518-457-4480
Web Page: www.dec.state.ny.us/
E-mail: fwwildlf@gw.dec.state.ny.us

| Resident | Non-Resident |
| --- | --- |
| Bear | Bear |
| Whitetail Deer | Whitetail Deer |

Deer and bear licenses are available over the counter. Whitetail deer are found statewide, with bear present only in the mountainous regions. Hunters may harvest one deer and one bear, with additional permits for antlerless deer available in some areas. Deer and bear seasons are controlled by Wildlife Management Units. Hunting methods are also restricted by Wildlife Management Unit, with some units open for archery hunting only, some open to archery, muzzleloader, shotguns, and handguns, and some open to archery, muzzleloader, shotguns, handguns, and rifles. Hunters buying their first New York license are required to have a Hunter Safety Card or a previous hunting license. Bowhunters are required to have a bowhunter education card. Regulations are available on-line. New York has more than 80 Wildlife Management Areas covering more than 170,000 acres. More than 3.6 million acres of state forests and preserves are also available to hunters without access to private property. Their web page allows hunters to access information on the Wildlife Management Areas and includes tract size, general directions and location maps, and permitted activities.

## Seasons

**Archery** - New York's archery deer seasons start in late September and run through late October in the northern units. Southern units start in mid-October and run through late November, with a second segment in mid-December. Deer of either sex may be taken in most units. Two counties are designated "Archery Only" and have a season starting in early November and running through December. Archery bear seasons vary by unit, with seasons open from late September through mid-December and varying in length from 26 to 41 days.

**Muzzleloader** - Most of the state is open to muzzleloader hunting and deer of either sex or antlerless only being legal game. Northern units typically have a seven-day season in mid to late October. Southern units have a seven-day season in mid to late December. Muzzleloader bear seasons are held in either mid-October or mid-December.

**Firearms** - Firearms deer seasons start in late-October and extend through early December in most northern units. Seasons in southern units are typically held from late November through mid-December. Bear seasons start in mid-September and run through mid-December and vary in length from 16 to 43 days.

## Suggestions

The Adirondack Mountains probably offer the best bear hunting in the state, and with overlapping seasons, a combination deer and bear hunt is a good way to enjoy your hunting time. With good access to some large lakes, hunters can use a boat or canoe to get to more remote areas and get away from some of the hunting pressure. Stillwater Reservoir is a good prospect for a boat-based hunt.

# Pennsylvania

Pennsylvania Game Department
2001 Elmerton Avenue
Harrisburg, PA 17110

Telephone: 717-787-4250
Web Page: www.pgc.state.pa.us/
E-mail: Not Available

| Resident | Non-Resident |
|---|---|
| Bear | Bear |
| Whitetail Deer | Whitetail Deer |

Deer and bear licenses are available over the counter for most of the state. Special regulations and seasons apply in select counties. Whitetail deer are found statewide and bears are found in the mountainous regions. Deer bag limits are based on hunting methods and license type. Hunters must purchase a special antlerless license to harvest antlerless deer. Muzzleloaders must be flintlock to hunt during the muzzleloader season. Semi-automatic firearms are prohibited. All hunters are required to have a Hunter Safety Card or a previous hunting license. Regulations and harvest information is available on-line. Hunting is prohibited on Sunday.

Pennsylvania has more than 300 tracts of State Game land totaling more than 1.4 million acres for public hunting. Combined with 4.5 million acres available through three cooperative programs and 19 State Forests covering millions of acres, hunters have outstanding public-land opportunities. Pennsylvania's web page contains links allowing hunters to access State Forest information.

## Seasons

**Archery** - Pennsylvania has split archery seasons with the first season typically starting in late September and running through mid-October. The second season starts in late October and extends through mid-November. The third season starts either in late December and runs through mid January. Seasons vary for antlered and antlerless deer.

**Muzzleloader** - There are typically two muzzleloader seasons - an early 3-day antlerless only season in late October and an either sex hunt in late December through mid-January. Flintlock muzzleloaders are the only legal muzzleloader for these seasons.

**Firearms** - Firearms deer season is typically held from late November until early December. There is typically an antlerless season during the last portion of the season, with a special license required to harvest antlerless deer.

Bear season is typically three days and is held in late November.

## Suggestions

With lots of public land available for hunting and archery seasons open during the rut, I suggest an archery hunt on State Forest land. Many of these tracts are large enough to offer solitude for hunters willing to work hard. Hunting during the rut provides increased deer movement and a better chance at a mature buck. Hunters might want to consider a bear hunt in Clearfield, Centre, or Clinton counties. These counties all have high bear numbers, lots of public land, and a good harvest.

# Rhode Island

Rhode Island Division of Fish & Wildlife
4808 Tower Hill Road
Wakefield, RI 02879

Telephone: 401-789-3094
Web Page: www.state.ri.us/dem/org/fish&w.htm
E-mail: Available through web page

| Resident | Non-Resident |
| --- | --- |
| Whitetail Deer | Whitetail Deer |

Deer seasons are established statewide, with some counties having additional opportunities on private property. Limits are typically 1 deer of either sex for each season - archery, muzzleloader, and firearms. A second deer of either sex may be taken on private lands in most areas. Rhode Island offers numerous hunts specifically for handicapped hunters. Hunters are restricted to shotguns only during the firearm seasons.

Rhode Island has numerous State Management Areas. Most are open to deer hunting - special restrictions may apply.

## Seasons

**Archery** - Rhode Island's archery deer season starts in early October and typically extends through the end of January. Hunters may take one deer (either sex) statewide and a second deer of either sex in specific areas.

**Muzzleloader** - The muzzleloader season starts in early November and runs through late November. Hunters may take one deer (either sex) and a second deer of either sex on private land.

**Firearms** - Firearms season is typically 9 days in length and opens in early December and closes in mid-December. Private land seasons in select counties extend another 5 days. Hunters may take one deer (either sex) and a second deer (either sex) on private property.

## Suggestions

Rhode Island has a program in the northwestern portion of the state called the Northwest Cooperative Program. This allows hunters access to private property and is an excellent opportunity for hunters without other access to private land. Special requirements apply to this program.

# Vermount

Vermont Fish and Wildlife Department
103 South Main Street
Waterbury, VT 05671

Telephone: 802-241-3700
Web Page: www.anr.state.vt.us/fw/fwhome/
E-mail: Not Available

| Resident | Non-Resident |
|---|---|
| Bear | Bear |
| Whitetail Deer | Whitetail Deer |

All deer and bear licenses are available over the counter. Whitetail deer and bears are found statewide. Vermont's web page has maps and descriptions of the 87 Wildlife Management Areas available. Information available includes habitat descriptions, wildlife species present, near-by facilities, etc.

## Seasons

**Archery** - Archery season for deer occurs in October, with a second segment coinciding with the muzzleloader season.

**Muzzleloader** - The muzzleloader season for deer is held in early December and usually runs 9 days.

**Firearms** - Firearms deer season is typically held in mid to late November and typically runs for 16 days. Firearms bear season runs from early September through mid-November.

## Suggestions

Vermont enjoys a strong deer population and a stable bear population. With good public access and a good variety of upland game, I recommend a combination archery hunt for deer and grouse. Most of the bear are taken earlier in the season as they feed before going to den for the winter. An early season hunt for bear would also provide an opportunity to view the fall colors and enjoy some of the best weather of the year.

Virginia Department of Game and Inland Fisheries
4010 West Broad Street
Richmond, VA 23230

Telephone: 804-367-1000
Web Page: www.dgif.state.va.us/index.cfm
E-mail: dgifweb@dgif.state.va.us

| Resident | Non-Resident |
|---|---|
| Bear | Bear |
| Whitetail Deer | Whitetail Deer |

Deer licenses are available over the counter, with drawings held for special hunts. Seasons are set for areas east and west of the Blue Ridge. Bag limits are set by county. Whitetail deer are found statewide, with bears present in many counties. Hunters may take from three to four deer per year, depending on area. Antlerless deer harvest is controlled through "either sex" days established for each county. The number of either sex days varies from one to 27. There are some restrictions on legal weapons in certain counties. Dogs may be used to hunt deer and bear, subject to specific restrictions.

Hunters between 12 and 15 years old are required to have a Hunter Safety Card. Older hunters are required to either certify that they have had a previous hunting license or have a Hunter Safety Card. Regulations are available online. Licenses may be bought through the mail. Virginia has 29 Wildlife Management Areas, numerous State Parks and State Forests, National Wildlife Refuges, Military Bases, and National Forests providing millions of acres of public hunting opportunity. Virginia's web page allows hunters to access Wildlife Management Area information including descriptions, maps, size, species present and special regulations. Hunting is prohibited on Sundays.

## Seasons

**Archery** - Virginia's archery deer season is typically divided into early and late segments - the early segment starts in early October and extends through mid-November and the late segment starts in early December and runs through the early January. Archery bear season starts in mid-October and runs through mid-November.

**Muzzleloader** - Muzzleloader deer seasons provide early and late season opportunities west of the Blue Ridge and an early opportunity east of the Blue Ridge. The early seasons are held in early to mid-November. The late season is held from mid-December through early January.

**Firearms** - Firearm deer seasons are typically held in late November through early December or early January, depending on location. Some counties west of Blue Ridge have a firearms season from early October through November.

## Suggestions

Virginia's Wildlife Management Areas offer excellent hunting. Hunting the Appalachian Mountains is an enjoyable experience and three Wildlife Management Areas offer great opportunities. The 14,000+ acre Highland Wildlife Management Area offers good deer and bear hunting, especially on the Jack Mountain tract. The Clinch Mountain Wildlife Management Area also offers over 25,000 acres of good deer and bear hunting. The largest Wildlife Management Area - Goshen-Little North Mountain and adjoining George Washington National Forest offer hunters good access to quality deer and bear habitat. With lots of walk-in hunting areas and some rugged terrain, hunters can get away from the crowds and enjoy the solitude

West Virginia Department of Natural Resources
State Capital Complex, Building #3
1900 Kanawha Blvd.
Charleston, WV 25305

Telephone: 304-558-2771
Web Page: www.dnr.state.wv.us/
E-mail: wildlife@dnr.state.wv.us

| Resident | Non-Resident |
|---|---|
| Bear | Bear |
| Whitetail Deer | Whitetail Deer |

Deer and bear licenses are available over the counter. Seasons and bag limits are set statewide. Whitetail deer are found statewide, with bears present in many counties. Hunters may take up to nine deer per year, depending on area. Antlerless deer harvest is controlled through "either sex" days established for each county. Some counties are closed to firearm deer hunting. Dogs may be used to hunt bear in specific areas, subject to restrictions. Deer may be hunted using bait.

Hunters born on or after January 1, 1975 are required to have a Hunter Safety Card. Regulations are available on-line. West Virginia has 58 Wildlife Management Areas, nine State Forests, and two National Forests providing millions of acres of public hunting opportunity. West Virginia's web page allows hunters to access Wildlife Management Area information including descriptions, habitat, size, species present, and access information. Harvest information is available on-line and is presented by county. Hunting is prohibited on Sundays.

## Seasons

**Archery** - West Virginia's archery deer season typically starts in mid-October and extends through late December. Archery bear season starts in mid-October and runs through mid-November.

**Muzzleloader** - Muzzleloader deer season is held in mid-December.

**Firearms** - Firearm deer seasons are typically held in late November through early December. Antlerless deer seasons are set by county. Bear seasons are typically held in December, with durations varying by county.

## Suggestions

West Virginia offers excellent hunting, with lots of public land available. Three counties offer great bear hunting - Pocahontas, Randolf and Greenbrier. Try the Greenbrier State Forest or the Becky Creek Wildlife Management Area for good bear hunting. Deer hunting can be good in most counties although populations vary. The Monongahela National Forest offers good deer and bear hunting opportunities.

## U.S. Forest Service

The U.S. Forest Service manages more than 190 million acres in 46 states in the form of National Forests and National Grasslands. Much of this land is open for public hunting and is accessible. Their web page can be found at www.fs.fed.us/ and contains information and links to regional and forest specific maps and web pages. Nine regions manage all of the individual forests - contact information for each region is provided below. Maps and additional information can be obtained from each regional office and/or from specific forest offices.

MT, ID, ND, SD, WA - 25 Million acres

USDA Forest Service
Northern Region
200 E. Broadway
PO Box 7669
Missoula, MT 59807
406-329-3511
www.fs.fed.us/r1/

CO, WY, SD, NE - 25 Million acres

USDA Forest Service
Rocky Mountain Regional Office
P.O. Box 25127
Lakewood, CO 80225-0127
303-275-5350
www.fs.fed.us/r2/

AZ, NM, TX, OK - 20 Million acres

USDA Forest Service
Southwestern Region
517 Gold Ave. SW
Albuquerque, NM 87102
505-842-3292
www.fs.fed.us/r3/

UT, NV, WY, ID - 33 Million acres

USDA Forest Service
Intermountain Region
Federal Building
324 25th Street
Ogden, Utah 84401
801-625-5306
www.fs.fed.us/r4/

CA - 20 Million acres

USDA Forest Service
Pacific Southwest Region
1323 Club Drive
Vallejo, CA 94592
707-562-8737
www.fs.fed.us/r5/

OR, WA - 24 million

USDA Forest Service
Pacific Northwest Region
PO Box 3623, 333 SW First Avenue
Portland, Oregon 97208-3623
503-808-2971
www.fs.fed.us/r6/

AL, AR, FL, GA, KY, LA, MS, NC, OK, SC, TN, TX, VA -
13 Million acres

USDA Forest Service
Southern Region
1720 Peachtree Road, NW
Atlanta, GA 30309
404-347-4177
http://www.r8web.com/

IL, IN, ME, MI, MN, MO, NH, NY, OH, PA, VT, WI, WV -
12 Million acres

USDA Forest Service
Eastern Region
310 W. Wisconsin Avenue, Rm. 580
Milwaukee, WI 53203
414-297-3600
www.fs.fed.us/r9/

AK - 22 Million acres

USDA Forest Service
Alaska Region
Federal Office Building, 709 W. 9th Street
PO Box 21628,
Juneau, AK 99802-1628
907-586-8806
www.fs.fed.us/r10/

## Bureau of Land Management

The Department of Interior's Bureau of Land Management (BLM) is responsible for managing over 264 million acres of public land. This property is located primarily in 11 western states. Much of this property is open for public use, including hunting. A wide variety of habitats and wildlife species are present in these holdings. Antelope, deer, and elk are the most common big game animals found on BLM lands.

State BLM offices provide the best source of information regarding public use, access, special regulations, and maps. The table below provides contact information for each state office and the amount of BLM land in each state.

Alaska - 87 million acres

Bureau of Land Management
222 West 7th Ave #13
Anchorage, AK 99513
907-271-5076
www.ak.blm.gov/

Arizona - 14 million acres

Bureau of Land Management
222 North Central Ave.
Phoenix, AZ 85014
602-417-9200az
www.az.blm.gov/

California - 14.5 million acres

Bureau of Land Management
2800 Cottage Way Suite 1834
Sacramento, CO 95825
916-978-4400
www.ca.blm.gov/

Colorado - 8.3 million acres

Bureau of Land Management
2850 Youngfield Street
Lakewood, CO 80215
303-239-3600
www.co.blm.gov/

Idaho - 11.9 million acres

Bureau of Land Management
1387 South Vinnell Way
Boise, Idaho 83709-1657
208-373-4000
www.id.blm.gov/

Montana - 8 million acres

Bureau of Land Management
5001 Southgate Drive
P.O. Box 36800
Billings, Montana 59107
406-896-7000
www.mt.blm.gov/

Nevada - 48 million acres
Bureau of Land Management
1340 Financial Blvd.
Reno, NV 89502
775-861-6400
www.nv.blm.gov/

New Mexico - 12.8 million acres
Bureau of Land Management
1474 Rodeo Drive
Sante Fe, NM 87505
505-438-7400
www.nm.blm.gov/

Oregon - 15.7 million acres
Bureau of Land Management
PO Box 2965
Portland, OR 97208
503-952-6002
www.or.blm.gov/

Wyoming - 18.4 million acres
Bureau of Land Management
P.O. Box 1828,
Cheyenne, WY 82003
307-775-6256
www.wy.blm.gov/

Need more copies?
Makes a great gift
for all your hunting
buddies!!

ORDER FORM

Your Guide To Big Game Hunting ____ qty. x 14.95 = $_______
From Field To Feast ____ qty. x 19.95 = $_______
CO residents add 3% sales tax = $_______
Shipping and Handling = $_FREE_
Express Mail (optional)$3.20 = $_______
TOTAL = $_______

Name_______________________________________________

Address_____________________________________________

City ______________________________ State _____ Zip_________

Phone (Day) ________________ Phone(Night)________________

__ Check/Money order Enclosed
(Make checks payable to Purple Mountain Outdoor Specialists)

Bill MY : ___ VISA ___ Mastercard ___ AMEX

Card #__________________________________ Expires _______________

Signature ____________________________________________________

Mail Orders To : Purple Mountain Outdoor Specialists
P.O. Box 2835
Evergreen, CO 80437-2835
or call toll-free 1-877-679-1460 M-F,(9:00am-7:00pmMST)
or visit our web-site at www.PurpleMtnOs.com
Allow 4 to 6 weeks for FREE delivery.